CIAM: Customer Identity and Access Management: the complete guide

James Relington

DEDICATION

To all cybersecurity professionals. Your commitment to protecting access, enforcing governance, and navigating the complexities of identity management is invaluable. May this work serve as a guide and inspiration in your ongoing efforts to create a more secure and compliant future.

Identity Introduction to CIAM 9

The Evolution of Identity and Access Management 11

Key Concepts of CIAM 14

Why CIAM Matters for Businesses 17

CIAM vs. Traditional IAM 20

The Role of CIAM in Digital Transformation 24

CIAM and Customer Experience..27

Core Components of CIAM Solutions 31

Authentication Methods in CIAM 34

Single Sign-On (SSO) for Customer Identities 38

Multi-Factor Authentication (MFA) Strategies 42

Open Standards in CIAM: OAuth, OIDC, and SAML...............................46

Passwordless Authentication in CIAM...49

Social Login and Third-Party Authentication 52

Identity Federation and CIAM 56

Customer Identity Lifecycle Management......................................59

User Registration and Onboarding..62

Self-Service Account Management...66

Progressive Profiling for Better CX...69

Consent Management in CIAM..73

CIAM and Data Privacy Regulations 76

GDPR, CCPA, and Global Compliance 79

The Role of AI and ML in CIAM 82

Risk-Based Authentication and Fraud Prevention 85

CIAM and Adaptive Access Controls 89

Customer Identity Governance and Administration.............................92

Secure APIs and CIAM Integration 96

Customer Identity and Omnichannel Strategies 100

CIAM for Mobile and IoT Devices..103

The Future of Biometric Authentication 107

Decentralized Identity and Blockchain in CIAM................................111

Zero Trust and CIAM Alignment 114

The Role of CIAM in B2C, B2B, and B2E................................118

CIAM for Financial Services and Banking 121

CIAM for Retail and E-Commerce..125

CIAM for Healthcare and Telemedicine 129

CIAM Implementation Best Practices 132

Selecting the Right CIAM Vendor 136

Cloud-Based vs. On-Premises CIAM Solutions................................140

CIAM in the Context of Cybersecurity................................144

The Cost of Poor CIAM Implementation................................148

The Role of CIAM in Customer Retention................................151

Case Studies: Successful CIAM Implementations 154

Common Pitfalls and How to Avoid Them................................158

Measuring CIAM Success: KPIs and Metrics................................161

The Future of CIAM: Trends and Predictions 165

How CIAM Supports Digital Identity Ecosystems................................169

CIAM and Customer Trust: Building a Secure Relationship 172

Automating CIAM Processes for Scalability 176

Final Thoughts: The Road Ahead for CIAM 179

AKNOWLEDGEMENTS

I extend my deepest gratitude to everyone who contributed to the creation of this book. To my colleagues and mentors in the field of identity governance, your insights and expertise have been invaluable. To my friends and family, your unwavering support and encouragement have made this journey possible. To the professionals and innovators dedicated to securing digital identities, your work continues to inspire and shape the future of cybersecurity. This book is a reflection of collective knowledge, and I am grateful to all who have played a role in its development.

Identity Introduction to CIAM

Customer Identity and Access Management (CIAM) is a critical component of modern digital ecosystems, enabling businesses to manage, secure, and optimize customer interactions while balancing security, usability, and regulatory compliance. As organizations increasingly shift toward digital-first strategies, the need for a robust CIAM framework has become more important than ever.

At its core, CIAM focuses on managing customer identities, providing seamless access to digital services, and ensuring a secure and personalized user experience. Unlike traditional Identity and Access Management (IAM) systems that primarily address internal users such as employees and contractors, CIAM is designed specifically for external users—customers, partners, and other stakeholders who interact with an organization's digital platforms. This distinction is crucial because customer interactions require a frictionless yet secure experience to maintain trust and engagement.

One of the primary goals of CIAM is to facilitate easy registration and authentication while ensuring strong security measures. Businesses need to strike a balance between security and user convenience, as excessive security barriers can drive customers away. To achieve this balance, modern CIAM solutions incorporate technologies such as Single Sign-On (SSO), Multi-Factor Authentication (MFA), passwordless authentication, and biometric verification. These features enhance security while maintaining a smooth user experience.

Another fundamental aspect of CIAM is identity federation, which allows customers to use a single identity across multiple platforms and services. This capability is particularly useful in ecosystems where customers interact with multiple brands or services under the same corporate umbrella. By leveraging identity federation, organizations can simplify user access while maintaining centralized control over security and compliance.

In addition to authentication and access control, CIAM plays a vital role in managing customer data. Organizations must collect, store, and process identity-related information responsibly, ensuring compliance with data protection regulations such as the General Data Protection

Regulation (GDPR) and the California Consumer Privacy Act (CCPA). Customers today expect transparency in how their data is used, and CIAM solutions help organizations implement proper consent management mechanisms to meet these expectations.

Another key component of CIAM is progressive profiling, which allows businesses to collect customer information gradually instead of requiring extensive data entry at the time of registration. This approach improves user experience by reducing initial friction and encourages users to provide more information over time as they engage with a brand's services. Progressive profiling also enables businesses to personalize interactions and deliver targeted content or recommendations based on user behavior and preferences.

Security is a major concern in any identity management system, and CIAM solutions incorporate advanced threat detection and risk-based authentication mechanisms to protect user accounts from fraud and unauthorized access. By leveraging artificial intelligence and machine learning, CIAM platforms can analyze user behavior in real-time, identifying suspicious activities and triggering additional verification steps when necessary. This proactive approach enhances security without compromising user convenience.

One of the biggest challenges organizations face when implementing CIAM is integrating it with existing systems. Many businesses operate legacy applications that were not built with modern identity management principles in mind. Ensuring seamless integration across various platforms, including mobile apps, web applications, and third-party services, requires a flexible and scalable CIAM solution. Open standards such as OAuth, OpenID Connect (OIDC), and Security Assertion Markup Language (SAML) facilitate interoperability and allow businesses to implement CIAM in a way that works with their existing infrastructure.

As the digital landscape continues to evolve, so do the expectations of customers regarding identity management. Users demand greater control over their personal information, the ability to manage their privacy settings, and the option to access services seamlessly across different devices. CIAM solutions must adapt to these changing demands by offering self-service account management, transparent data policies, and enhanced user privacy controls.

Beyond security and usability, CIAM also has a direct impact on business success. A well-implemented CIAM strategy can drive customer acquisition, increase engagement, and improve retention rates. By providing a seamless login experience, businesses can reduce abandonment rates, especially in e-commerce and subscription-based services where a complicated authentication process can lead to lost

The Evolution of Identity and Access Management

Identity and Access Management (IAM) has undergone significant transformation over the years, evolving from simple password-based authentication to complex, AI-driven security frameworks. As digital landscapes have expanded, organizations have faced increasing challenges in securing identities while maintaining a seamless user experience. The history of IAM reflects broader shifts in technology, security threats, and user expectations, making it an essential component of modern business operations.

In the early days of computing, identity management was a relatively simple concept. Users were assigned unique usernames and passwords to access systems, typically within closed networks. These credentials were manually created and managed by IT administrators, who controlled access based on predefined roles and permissions. While this approach worked in small, isolated environments, it quickly became inefficient as organizations grew and adopted more digital systems. Managing user access manually led to errors, security risks, and inefficiencies, highlighting the need for a more structured approach.

As businesses expanded their digital presence, the first wave of IAM solutions emerged in the form of centralized authentication systems. These systems allowed organizations to manage user identities from a single point of control, reducing administrative burdens and improving security. However, authentication remained largely static, relying primarily on passwords. As cyber threats became more sophisticated, attackers exploited weak and reused passwords, leading to a surge in security breaches. This prompted organizations to explore stronger authentication methods.

The introduction of multi-factor authentication (MFA) marked a major step forward in identity security. By requiring users to verify their identity using multiple factors—such as something they know (password), something they have (security token), or something they are (biometrics)—organizations significantly reduced the risk of unauthorized access. MFA became a standard security measure, especially in industries handling sensitive data, such as finance and healthcare.

With the rise of the internet and cloud computing, identity management had to evolve beyond traditional corporate networks. Employees, customers, and partners needed to access systems from anywhere, on any device. This shift led to the development of federated identity management, which enabled users to authenticate once and gain access to multiple systems without needing separate credentials. Standards such as Security Assertion Markup Language (SAML) and later OpenID Connect (OIDC) facilitated interoperability across different platforms, allowing organizations to implement Single Sign-On (SSO) for improved user convenience and security.

As digital transformation accelerated, organizations recognized the need for customer-centric identity solutions. Traditional IAM systems were designed for internal users, but businesses now required scalable identity solutions for millions of customers. This gave rise to Customer Identity and Access Management (CIAM), which focused on balancing security with a seamless user experience. Unlike traditional IAM, CIAM emphasized self-service registration, social logins, consent management, and progressive profiling to enhance customer engagement while maintaining security compliance.

Another critical milestone in IAM evolution was the adoption of risk-based authentication and adaptive security measures. Instead of relying on static authentication policies, modern IAM systems analyze real-time risk factors—such as login location, device type, and behavioral patterns—to determine the appropriate level of authentication. This adaptive approach allows businesses to strengthen security without creating unnecessary friction for legitimate users. If a login attempt appears suspicious, additional verification steps are triggered, while low-risk interactions proceed seamlessly.

The increasing sophistication of cyber threats, including phishing attacks and credential stuffing, drove the adoption of passwordless authentication methods. Traditional passwords were no longer sufficient to protect user identities, leading to the rise of biometrics, hardware security keys, and authentication apps. Passwordless authentication not only enhances security but also improves user experience by eliminating the need to remember complex passwords.

With the emergence of artificial intelligence and machine learning, IAM solutions have become more intelligent and proactive. AI-driven IAM can detect anomalies, predict potential security threats, and automate access decisions based on contextual data. Machine learning models continuously improve by analyzing user behavior patterns, making IAM more effective at preventing fraud and unauthorized access. These advancements have made IAM a cornerstone of Zero Trust security frameworks, where no entity is trusted by default, and continuous verification is required.

As the world moves towards a decentralized identity model, blockchain technology has begun influencing IAM strategies. Decentralized identity shifts control of personal data from centralized authorities to individual users, allowing them to manage their own credentials securely. This approach enhances privacy and reduces the risk of large-scale data breaches, as sensitive identity information is not stored in a single location.

The evolution of IAM reflects broader technological advancements and shifting security challenges. From simple passwords to AI-powered, decentralized identity systems, IAM has continuously adapted to meet the needs of modern organizations and users. Today, IAM is not just a security measure but a fundamental enabler of digital transformation, customer trust, and regulatory compliance. As technology continues to evolve, identity and access management will remain at the forefront of digital security and user experience innovation.

Key Concepts of CIAM

Customer Identity and Access Management (CIAM) is a specialized branch of identity and access management designed to handle customer identities in a secure, scalable, and user-friendly manner. Unlike traditional IAM systems that focus on internal users such as employees and contractors, CIAM is centered on customers, providing seamless authentication, authorization, and personalized experiences across digital platforms. Understanding the key concepts of CIAM is essential for organizations looking to enhance security while optimizing the customer experience.

One of the fundamental principles of CIAM is authentication, the process of verifying a user's identity before granting access to a service. Traditional authentication methods rely on usernames and passwords, but passwords alone are no longer sufficient to protect customer identities. CIAM systems incorporate advanced authentication mechanisms such as multi-factor authentication (MFA), passwordless login, biometrics, and risk-based authentication to strengthen security while minimizing friction for legitimate users. These methods ensure that customers can securely access their accounts without unnecessary complexity.

Single Sign-On (SSO) is another key concept within CIAM. It enables customers to authenticate once and gain access to multiple applications or services without the need to enter credentials repeatedly. This not only enhances the user experience but also reduces the risk of password fatigue and security breaches. By leveraging identity federation standards such as OAuth, OpenID Connect (OIDC), and SAML, CIAM platforms allow users to move seamlessly across different platforms while maintaining a single identity.

Customer registration and onboarding processes are also critical aspects of CIAM. A well-designed registration system ensures that users can create accounts easily while maintaining compliance with security and regulatory requirements. CIAM platforms often support social login, allowing users to sign up using their existing accounts from providers such as Google, Facebook, or Apple. This simplifies the onboarding process and reduces the need for users to remember additional credentials. Progressive profiling is another strategy used in CIAM, enabling businesses to collect customer data gradually rather than requiring extensive information at the time of registration. This reduces friction and encourages users to engage with the platform over time.

Consent and privacy management play a crucial role in modern CIAM systems. With increasing global regulations such as GDPR and CCPA, businesses must ensure that customer data is collected, stored, and processed in compliance with privacy laws. CIAM solutions include mechanisms for users to provide, review, and manage their consent preferences, ensuring transparency and trust. Customers must have the ability to control their personal data, update their privacy settings, and request data deletion when necessary.

Authorization, the process of determining what a user is allowed to do after authentication, is another key CIAM concept. Role-based access control (RBAC) and attribute based access control (ABAC) are commonly used to enforce authorization policies. In a customer-centric environment, dynamic authorization models are often required to provide personalized experiences based on user behavior, preferences, or purchase history. CIAM platforms integrate with backend systems to ensure that access policies align with business goals while maintaining security.

Scalability is a defining characteristic of CIAM solutions. Unlike traditional IAM systems that manage a limited number of employee identities, CIAM must support millions of customers accessing digital services across different geographies and devices. Cloud-based CIAM solutions offer the flexibility to handle high volumes of authentication requests while maintaining low latency and high availability. Auto-scaling capabilities ensure that customer experiences remain smooth even during peak usage periods, such as major sales events or product launches.

Fraud prevention and risk-based authentication are essential components of CIAM. As cyber threats continue to evolve, businesses must implement intelligent security measures to detect and prevent fraudulent activities. CIAM platforms leverage artificial intelligence and machine learning to analyze user behavior patterns, identify anomalies, and trigger additional verification steps when suspicious activity is detected. This adaptive approach enhances security without disrupting legitimate users.

Interoperability and integration with existing systems are also key considerations in CIAM. Businesses often operate a diverse technology stack that includes web applications, mobile apps, APIs, and third-party services. CIAM solutions must be compatible with various authentication protocols and identity providers to ensure seamless integration. Open standards such as OAuth 2.0 enable secure API access, allowing businesses to extend identity management capabilities across their entire digital ecosystem.

Another important aspect of CIAM is omnichannel identity management. Customers expect a consistent and seamless experience across multiple touchpoints, including websites, mobile apps, kiosks, and customer service interactions. CIAM enables organizations to provide a unified identity experience, ensuring that customers can log in once and access services across different channels without disruptions. By centralizing identity data, businesses can personalize interactions, offer targeted recommendations, and improve overall customer engagement.

Security and compliance are at the core of every CIAM strategy. Organizations must implement strong identity verification processes, encrypt sensitive customer data, and adhere to industry-specific regulations. Regular security audits, penetration testing, and adherence to best practices help prevent data breaches and build customer trust. CIAM platforms also support logging and monitoring capabilities to track access patterns, detect unauthorized activities, and generate compliance reports.

By combining security, convenience, and scalability, CIAM enables businesses to build trusted relationships with their customers while protecting sensitive identity information. As digital transformation accelerates, organizations must continuously adapt their CIAM strategies to address evolving threats, regulatory requirements, and customer expectations. A well-implemented CIAM solution not only enhances security but also drives customer loyalty and business growth.

Why CIAM Matters for Businesses

Customer Identity and Access Management (CIAM) has become a fundamental component of modern digital business strategies. As companies continue to expand their online presence, managing customer identities securely while ensuring a seamless user experience is critical. CIAM is not just about authentication and authorization; it is a strategic enabler that helps businesses drive customer engagement, improve security, and ensure regulatory compliance.

One of the most significant reasons CIAM matters for businesses is its impact on customer experience. In a highly competitive digital landscape, customers expect frictionless interactions across multiple platforms and devices. A complicated or frustrating login experience can drive users away, leading to lost revenue and decreased brand loyalty. CIAM solutions enable businesses to provide smooth authentication methods, including Single Sign-On (SSO), social login, and passwordless authentication, making it easier for customers to access services without unnecessary barriers.

Security is another major reason why businesses need CIAM. Cyber threats, such as account takeovers, credential stuffing, and identity fraud, pose serious risks to companies handling customer data. A robust CIAM system incorporates multi-factor authentication (MFA), risk-based authentication, and real-time threat detection to protect user accounts from unauthorized access. By implementing strong identity security measures, businesses can reduce fraud, prevent data breaches, and safeguard customer trust.

Regulatory compliance is a growing concern for businesses operating in multiple regions. Laws such as the General Data Protection Regulation (GDPR), the California Consumer Privacy Act (CCPA), and other privacy regulations require companies to manage customer data responsibly. CIAM platforms help businesses meet compliance requirements by providing features such as consent management, data encryption, and audit logs. These capabilities ensure that businesses can demonstrate accountability in handling customer identities while avoiding hefty fines and legal penalties.

Scalability is another critical factor that makes CIAM essential for businesses. Unlike traditional IAM systems designed for managing a limited number of employee identities, CIAM solutions must accommodate millions of customer identities across various touchpoints. During peak periods, such as holiday shopping seasons or major product launches, businesses experience high volumes of authentication requests. A well-implemented CIAM solution ensures that these spikes in demand do not lead to service disruptions, providing a reliable and consistent user experience.

Personalization is increasingly becoming a key differentiator in customer engagement. Businesses that understand their customers' behaviors and preferences can offer tailored experiences that enhance customer satisfaction and increase revenue. CIAM enables businesses to collect and manage customer data in a way that supports personalized marketing, recommendations, and targeted offers. By leveraging progressive profiling, businesses can gather additional customer information over time, improving their ability to deliver relevant content and services.

Customer retention is another area where CIAM plays a crucial role. Studies have shown that users are more likely to remain loyal to a brand that provides a secure and convenient digital experience. A seamless authentication process, combined with strong security measures, reassures customers that their data is protected, increasing trust and long-term engagement. Businesses that prioritize CIAM can reduce churn rates and improve customer lifetime value by offering a frictionless yet secure experience.

Omnichannel access is becoming an expectation rather than a luxury. Customers interact with brands across websites, mobile apps, IoT devices, and even smart assistants. CIAM ensures that users have a unified identity across all these channels, allowing them to switch between devices without losing their session or having to reauthenticate repeatedly. This level of convenience enhances customer satisfaction and encourages continued engagement with the brand.

The growing reliance on APIs and third-party integrations makes CIAM even more critical for businesses. Many companies rely on external partners, payment gateways, and service providers to deliver a complete customer experience. CIAM enables secure API authentication and access management, ensuring that customer identities remain protected while integrating with third-party services. Open standards such as OAuth 2.0 and OpenID Connect (OIDC) allow businesses to extend authentication capabilities without compromising security.

Fraud prevention is a key advantage of CIAM. Businesses that operate in industries such as e-commerce, financial services, and healthcare face a constant battle against identity fraud. CIAM solutions incorporate machine learning and AI-driven risk assessment to identify suspicious behavior patterns, detect anomalies, and trigger additional security measures when necessary. By implementing adaptive authentication, businesses can prevent fraudulent transactions without creating unnecessary friction for legitimate customers.

Business continuity and disaster recovery are often overlooked aspects of identity management. A well-architected CIAM solution ensures that customer authentication and access processes remain operational even in the face of cyberattacks, system failures, or data breaches. By implementing redundant and distributed authentication services, businesses can minimize downtime and maintain trust with their customers.

Brand reputation is closely tied to how businesses handle customer identities. A data breach or a poorly executed authentication experience can significantly damage a company's reputation, leading to loss of customer trust and negative publicity. CIAM allows businesses to proactively protect user identities, ensuring that they remain compliant with security best practices while delivering a seamless user experience. Companies that prioritize CIAM demonstrate their commitment to security and customer privacy, strengthening their brand image in the marketplace.

By investing in CIAM, businesses position themselves for long-term success in the digital economy. The ability to provide secure, seamless, and scalable identity management enhances customer engagement, reduces security risks, and ensures compliance with evolving regulations. Organizations that integrate CIAM effectively into their digital strategies gain a competitive edge, building stronger relationships with customers while protecting sensitive data from emerging threats.

CIAM vs. Traditional IAM

Identity and Access Management (IAM) has long been a fundamental aspect of enterprise security, ensuring that only authorized users have access to the right resources at the right time. As businesses have evolved to serve digital customers at scale, a new approach to identity management has emerged—Customer Identity and Access Management (CIAM). While traditional IAM solutions are designed primarily for managing internal employees and corporate assets, CIAM is tailored to meet the unique needs of external users such as customers, partners, and vendors. Understanding the differences between these two identity management approaches is critical for organizations looking to enhance security while delivering seamless digital experiences.

Traditional IAM solutions were developed to control employee access within corporate environments. These systems typically focus on managing identities within an organization's internal network, ensuring that users can access enterprise applications, databases, and other resources based on their roles and responsibilities. Traditional IAM operates under strict governance policies, enforcing access controls through role-based access control (RBAC) and identity lifecycle management. Employee identities are created, modified, and deactivated based on their employment status, ensuring that access is granted only when necessary.

CIAM, on the other hand, is designed to manage identities beyond the corporate firewall. Unlike traditional IAM, which serves a fixed number of employees, CIAM solutions must accommodate millions of customer identities across various platforms and devices. Customer interactions require a balance between security and user experience, making CIAM more flexible and user-friendly compared to traditional IAM. Since customer identities are not managed by internal IT teams in the same way as employee identities, CIAM solutions prioritize self-service registration, seamless authentication, and user consent management.

Authentication methods differ significantly between traditional IAM and CIAM. In an enterprise IAM system, employees typically authenticate using a username and password, often combined with multi-factor authentication (MFA) for added security. These authentication processes are rigid, designed to enforce corporate security policies. In contrast, CIAM solutions offer a variety of authentication options to improve user convenience. Customers can log in using social media accounts, biometric authentication, or passwordless methods such as one-time passcodes (OTPs) or magic links. Since customer expectations for convenience are high, CIAM systems must support authentication flows that minimize friction while maintaining strong security.

Another key distinction between traditional IAM and CIAM is the way identities are managed and stored. In traditional IAM, identity management is centralized within an organization's IT infrastructure, often integrated with corporate directories such as Active Directory (AD) or Lightweight Directory Access Protocol (LDAP) servers. These directories store employee credentials, group memberships, and access rights, which are controlled by internal administrators. CIAM, however, is built on cloud-based, scalable architectures that allow businesses to handle large volumes of customer identities efficiently. Instead of relying on static directory structures, CIAM solutions utilize dynamic identity stores that support federated authentication, customer consent tracking, and personalized user profiles.

Customer experience plays a significant role in the design of CIAM systems. Traditional IAM systems are optimized for security and compliance, often requiring strict password policies and periodic access reviews. Employees are accustomed to these security measures as part of their workplace requirements. However, customers expect a frictionless experience when accessing online services. CIAM solutions emphasize progressive profiling, allowing businesses to collect user data gradually instead of forcing customers to fill out lengthy registration forms upfront. This approach enhances user engagement while enabling businesses to personalize customer interactions over time.

Regulatory compliance requirements also differ between traditional IAM and CIAM. While enterprise IAM focuses on internal security policies, CIAM solutions must comply with global privacy regulations such as the General Data Protection Regulation (GDPR), the California Consumer Privacy Act (CCPA), and other data protection laws. These regulations mandate that businesses obtain customer consent for data collection, provide transparency regarding how personal information is used, and offer users the ability to manage their privacy preferences. CIAM platforms include built-in consent management features that allow customers to opt in or out of data sharing, ensuring compliance with evolving privacy laws.

Scalability is another critical factor that distinguishes CIAM from traditional IAM. In a corporate setting, IAM systems are designed to handle a relatively stable number of users, typically in the thousands. Employee access patterns are predictable, and IAM solutions can be structured around organizational hierarchies. CIAM, however, must support millions of customer identities with unpredictable access patterns. During peak periods, such as holiday sales or major product launches, authentication requests can spike dramatically. CIAM platforms leverage cloud-based architectures with auto-scaling capabilities to ensure high availability and performance under heavy traffic loads.

Security risks in traditional IAM and CIAM also differ due to the nature of user interactions. Employees operate within controlled environments, using company-issued devices and accessing corporate networks through secured VPNs or enterprise firewalls. In contrast, customers access digital services from a variety of personal devices, browsers, and locations. CIAM solutions incorporate advanced security measures such as risk-based authentication, device fingerprinting, and behavioral analytics to detect suspicious activities. By analyzing login behavior, geolocation, and device information, CIAM platforms can identify potential fraud and enforce additional verification steps only when necessary.

Integration capabilities further set CIAM apart from traditional IAM. Enterprise IAM solutions are typically integrated with internal business applications such as email systems, HR platforms, and enterprise resource planning (ERP) software. These integrations focus on streamlining employee access to work-related resources. CIAM, however, must integrate with a wide range of customer-facing applications, including mobile apps, e-commerce platforms, customer support portals, and third-party identity providers. Open standards such as OAuth, OpenID Connect (OIDC), and Security Assertion Markup Language (SAML) enable CIAM solutions to provide seamless authentication across multiple digital ecosystems.

Organizations that rely solely on traditional IAM solutions for customer interactions often face challenges in delivering smooth user experiences. While traditional IAM is well-suited for securing internal users, it lacks the scalability, flexibility, and customer-centric features required for modern digital businesses. CIAM bridges this gap by providing a comprehensive identity management framework that enhances security while optimizing customer engagement. As businesses continue to evolve in an increasingly digital world, adopting a CIAM solution becomes essential for building secure and frictionless online experiences.

The Role of CIAM in Digital Transformation

Digital transformation is reshaping the way businesses operate, interact with customers, and deliver value. Organizations across industries are leveraging technology to streamline processes, enhance user experiences, and stay competitive in an increasingly digital-first world. Customer Identity and Access Management (CIAM) plays a crucial role in this transformation by providing the foundation for secure, seamless, and personalized interactions across digital platforms. As businesses move towards a more connected and data-driven ecosystem, CIAM becomes an essential enabler of innovation, security, and customer trust.

A fundamental aspect of digital transformation is the shift towards online and mobile-first engagement. Consumers expect instant access to services from any device, at any time, without unnecessary friction. CIAM enables businesses to offer frictionless authentication and access management, allowing customers to log in easily using Single Sign-On (SSO), social login, or passwordless authentication. By eliminating barriers to access, businesses enhance customer satisfaction and drive higher engagement.

Security is a key concern in digital transformation efforts. As organizations expand their digital footprint, they also become more vulnerable to cyber threats, identity theft, and data breaches. Traditional security measures, such as simple password-based authentication, are no longer sufficient to protect customer identities. CIAM solutions integrate advanced security mechanisms, including multi-factor authentication (MFA), risk-based authentication, and behavioral analytics, to protect user accounts from unauthorized access. These security measures help businesses mitigate risks while maintaining a seamless user experience.

Another critical component of digital transformation is data-driven decision-making. Organizations rely on customer data to personalize experiences, optimize marketing strategies, and improve service delivery. CIAM acts as the central hub for managing customer identities, collecting consented data, and ensuring compliance with privacy regulations. By integrating with customer relationship management (CRM) systems, analytics platforms, and artificial intelligence (AI) tools, CIAM enables businesses to gain deeper insights into customer behaviors, preferences, and engagement patterns. This data-driven approach allows organizations to deliver hyper-personalized experiences that increase customer loyalty and drive revenue growth.

Regulatory compliance is a significant challenge for businesses undergoing digital transformation. Data protection laws such as the General Data Protection Regulation (GDPR) and the California Consumer Privacy Act (CCPA) impose strict requirements on how organizations collect, store, and process customer information. CIAM solutions incorporate built-in consent management, data encryption, and access control features that help businesses meet compliance requirements. By providing customers with control over their personal data and preferences, businesses can build trust and demonstrate their commitment to privacy and security.

The scalability of CIAM solutions is another factor that makes them indispensable in digital transformation initiatives. Unlike traditional identity management systems designed for a limited number of internal users, CIAM is built to support millions of customers across multiple channels. Whether a business is a startup experiencing rapid growth or a large enterprise managing global operations, CIAM ensures that authentication and access management processes remain efficient and scalable. Cloud-based CIAM solutions allow businesses to handle high volumes of authentication requests, ensuring uninterrupted service even during peak traffic periods.

Omnichannel engagement is a core component of digital transformation, as customers interact with businesses through various touchpoints, including websites, mobile apps, IoT devices, and customer support portals. CIAM ensures a consistent and unified identity experience across all these channels, allowing users to access services seamlessly without needing to reauthenticate multiple times. By enabling cross-channel authentication and identity federation, businesses can deliver a cohesive digital experience that enhances customer satisfaction and retention.

Automation and artificial intelligence are accelerating digital transformation, and CIAM solutions are increasingly incorporating AI-driven capabilities to enhance security and usability. Machine learning algorithms can analyze login patterns, detect anomalies, and identify potential fraud in real time. By continuously learning from user behavior, AI-powered CIAM systems can dynamically adjust authentication requirements based on risk levels. This adaptive approach ensures that legitimate users can access services effortlessly while blocking suspicious activities before they escalate into security threats.

The role of CIAM extends beyond security and authentication; it also contributes to revenue generation and business growth. A well-implemented CIAM strategy reduces user abandonment rates by simplifying the login and registration process. Businesses that offer seamless authentication experiences see higher conversion rates, especially in e-commerce and subscription-based services. Additionally, CIAM enables businesses to implement targeted marketing campaigns by leveraging customer identity data to deliver personalized offers and recommendations.

In a competitive digital landscape, customer trust is a valuable asset. Organizations that prioritize identity security and privacy earn the confidence of their users, leading to stronger brand loyalty and long-term relationships. CIAM provides customers with transparency and control over their data, allowing them to manage privacy settings, consent preferences, and account security. By fostering trust through secure and ethical identity management practices, businesses can differentiate themselves from competitors and build lasting customer relationships.

As technology continues to evolve, businesses must adapt to emerging trends such as decentralized identity and blockchain-based authentication. CIAM solutions are evolving to support these innovations, enabling organizations to provide users with more control over their digital identities while reducing reliance on centralized identity providers. By embracing next-generation CIAM capabilities, businesses can future-proof their digital transformation strategies and stay ahead of industry disruptions.

The integration of CIAM with other digital transformation initiatives, such as cloud computing, API security, and IoT identity management, further enhances its value. Organizations that adopt a holistic approach to identity management can streamline operations, improve security posture, and deliver exceptional customer experiences. By embedding CIAM into their digital ecosystems, businesses can unlock new opportunities for innovation and growth.

CIAM is a critical enabler of digital transformation, providing businesses with the tools they need to manage customer identities securely, deliver personalized experiences, and comply with regulatory requirements. As organizations continue to evolve in a digital-first world, CIAM will remain a foundational component of their success.

CIAM and Customer Experience

Customer Identity and Access Management (CIAM) is a critical factor in shaping the overall customer experience. As businesses transition to digital-first interactions, the way customers access and engage with online services has a direct impact on their satisfaction, trust, and long-term loyalty. A seamless authentication and identity management process ensures that users can interact effortlessly with a brand while maintaining security and privacy. CIAM enables businesses to provide personalized, secure, and user-friendly experiences across multiple touchpoints.

One of the most noticeable ways CIAM influences customer experience is during the login and registration process. When customers visit a website or use a mobile application, the first interaction they have is often creating an account or logging in. A cumbersome, time-consuming process with lengthy forms and strict password requirements can deter potential users from completing their registration. CIAM solutions offer flexible authentication methods, including social login, passwordless authentication, and Single Sign-On (SSO), reducing friction and making access more convenient. A smooth onboarding experience increases the likelihood of users engaging with a service rather than abandoning it out of frustration.

Security is an essential aspect of customer experience, yet it must be balanced with usability. Customers want to feel confident that their personal information is protected, but they also expect quick and hassle-free access. Traditional authentication methods that require frequent password changes, complex password rules, and additional verification steps can create frustration. CIAM platforms use intelligent security measures such as risk-based authentication, adaptive MFA, and behavioral analytics to assess the risk level of a login attempt. If a user is logging in from a familiar device and location, the system may allow seamless access, whereas an unusual login attempt may trigger additional verification steps. This approach enhances security without disrupting the experience for legitimate users.

Personalization is another key benefit of CIAM in customer experience. Businesses collect customer data to provide tailored recommendations, targeted promotions, and customized content. A robust CIAM system enables organizations to securely manage and utilize this data while giving users control over their preferences. Progressive profiling allows businesses to collect information gradually rather than requiring customers to fill out extensive forms at once. By remembering user preferences, purchase history, and interactions across devices, CIAM solutions help businesses deliver a more personalized and engaging experience that keeps customers coming back.

Omnichannel consistency is increasingly important as customers interact with brands through websites, mobile apps, smart devices, and even customer support chatbots. CIAM ensures that customers can use a single identity across all platforms without needing to repeatedly authenticate themselves. A user who logs into a website on a laptop should be able to continue their session seamlessly on a mobile app without having to re-enter credentials. This consistency enhances convenience and strengthens brand loyalty by providing a unified experience across all digital touchpoints.

Consent and privacy management have become major concerns for customers in an era of increasing data breaches and privacy regulations. Customers expect transparency regarding how their data is used and the ability to control their privacy settings. CIAM platforms incorporate consent management features that allow users to grant, modify, or revoke permissions for data collection. Features such as self-service account management, privacy preference centers, and data access requests empower customers with control over their information. Businesses that prioritize user privacy build stronger relationships with customers and enhance their brand reputation.

Account recovery is another aspect of customer experience where CIAM plays a significant role. Forgotten passwords, locked accounts, and security challenges can lead to frustration and lost business opportunities. Traditional account recovery methods, such as answering security questions or waiting for email verification, can be time-consuming and insecure. CIAM solutions provide more efficient account recovery options, including biometric authentication, mobile push notifications, and passwordless authentication. By streamlining recovery processes, businesses reduce customer frustration and prevent users from abandoning their accounts due to login difficulties.

Fraud prevention is critical for maintaining a positive customer experience. Identity theft, account takeovers, and fraudulent transactions can severely damage customer trust. CIAM platforms incorporate fraud detection mechanisms that analyze login patterns, geolocation data, and device behavior to identify suspicious activity. If an unusual transaction or login attempt is detected, the system can prompt additional verification steps or block the request altogether. By proactively preventing fraud, businesses protect their customers while ensuring legitimate users can access their accounts without unnecessary disruptions.

Scalability is an important factor in delivering a consistent and reliable customer experience, especially for businesses with large user bases. Traditional IAM systems may struggle to handle high volumes of authentication requests during peak times, leading to slow logins, timeouts, or service disruptions. CIAM solutions are built to scale dynamically, ensuring that millions of users can log in simultaneously without performance issues. Whether during a major sales event, product launch, or viral campaign, businesses with a strong CIAM infrastructure can maintain a smooth and uninterrupted experience for their customers.

Seamless integration with third-party services is another advantage of CIAM in enhancing customer experience. Many businesses rely on external platforms for payments, support services, loyalty programs, and partner networks. A CIAM system enables secure and efficient integration with these services using open standards such as OAuth, OpenID Connect (OIDC), and Security Assertion Markup Language (SAML). This allows customers to navigate between different services without needing to create multiple accounts or remember additional credentials, creating a more convenient and cohesive digital experience.

Customer loyalty is heavily influenced by the quality of identity management and access experiences. A smooth, secure, and user-friendly authentication process encourages users to return to a platform and engage more frequently. When businesses fail to provide an intuitive login experience, customers may abandon the service in favor of competitors with better authentication systems. CIAM helps businesses retain users by ensuring fast access, strong security, and personalized interactions that align with customer expectations.

By implementing a robust CIAM strategy, businesses can significantly enhance customer experience while ensuring security, scalability, and regulatory compliance. Customers value effortless authentication, data privacy, and personalized engagement, all of which are made possible through a well-designed CIAM solution. Organizations that prioritize identity management as part of their digital experience strategy create stronger customer relationships, increase retention, and drive business growth in an increasingly competitive market.

Core Components of CIAM Solutions

Customer Identity and Access Management (CIAM) solutions are designed to handle customer authentication, authorization, and identity lifecycle management while ensuring security and a seamless user experience. Unlike traditional IAM systems that focus on internal employees, CIAM is built for scalability, flexibility, and user convenience. A comprehensive CIAM solution consists of multiple core components that work together to provide secure and efficient access to digital services.

Authentication is one of the fundamental components of CIAM. This process verifies a user's identity before granting access to applications and services. Traditional authentication methods, such as username and password combinations, are becoming less effective due to security risks and poor user experience. CIAM platforms incorporate advanced authentication mechanisms, including multi-factor authentication (MFA), biometric authentication, passwordless login, and social login. These methods reduce reliance on passwords while enhancing security and usability. Single Sign-On (SSO) further simplifies authentication by allowing users to log in once and gain access to multiple applications without re-entering credentials.

Authorization determines what a user can do once authenticated. CIAM solutions enforce access control policies that define permissions based on roles, attributes, or risk levels. Role-based access control (RBAC) assigns permissions based on predefined roles, while attribute-based access control (ABAC) evaluates user attributes such as location, device, and risk level before granting access. Dynamic authorization models use real-time context to make access decisions, ensuring that customers can securely interact with services while minimizing the risk of unauthorized access.

User registration and onboarding are crucial elements of the customer experience in CIAM. A well-designed registration process encourages user engagement while maintaining security. CIAM solutions support self-service registration, allowing users to create accounts quickly with minimal effort. Many platforms also offer social login, enabling users to sign up using existing credentials from providers like Google, Facebook, or Apple. Progressive profiling is another key feature, allowing businesses to collect additional user information over time rather than requiring extensive data entry during the initial registration process.

Identity federation enables users to access multiple services using a single identity. Businesses that operate multiple brands or partner ecosystems benefit from federated identity management, which allows customers to move between services without creating separate accounts. CIAM platforms use industry standards such as OAuth 2.0, OpenID Connect (OIDC), and Security Assertion Markup Language (SAML) to facilitate identity federation. These standards ensure interoperability between identity providers and service providers, enabling seamless cross-platform authentication.

Consent and privacy management are essential components of modern CIAM solutions. With growing data privacy regulations such as the General Data Protection Regulation (GDPR) and the California Consumer Privacy Act (CCPA), businesses must ensure that customer data is collected and processed with explicit consent. CIAM platforms include built-in consent management tools that allow users to review, modify, or withdraw their consent at any time. These solutions also support data access requests, enabling customers to manage their privacy preferences and comply with legal requirements.

Fraud detection and risk-based authentication enhance security by analyzing user behavior and contextual factors to identify potential threats. CIAM solutions leverage machine learning and artificial intelligence to detect anomalies such as unusual login attempts, multiple failed authentication attempts, and access from high-risk locations. When suspicious activity is detected, risk-based authentication dynamically adjusts security measures by requiring additional verification steps, such as an MFA prompt or biometric authentication. This proactive approach helps prevent account takeovers and fraudulent transactions while minimizing disruptions for legitimate users.

Scalability is a critical aspect of CIAM solutions, as businesses must accommodate millions of customers accessing services across different devices and locations. Traditional IAM systems were not designed for such high-volume, dynamic user bases. Cloud-based CIAM platforms provide elastic scalability, ensuring that authentication and identity management services remain responsive even during peak traffic periods. Auto-scaling capabilities help businesses maintain performance and availability while optimizing costs.

Omnichannel identity management allows users to maintain a consistent identity across multiple touchpoints, including web applications, mobile apps, IoT devices, and customer service portals. CIAM platforms centralize identity data, ensuring that customers can access services seamlessly without needing to reauthenticate across different channels. By integrating with customer engagement platforms, businesses can personalize interactions based on user preferences, location, and past behaviors.

Self-service account management empowers users to control their identity and security settings without relying on customer support. CIAM solutions provide user-friendly interfaces for updating personal information, managing passwords, configuring MFA settings, and reviewing account activity. Self-service features enhance user convenience while reducing operational costs associated with password resets and account recovery requests.

API security and integration capabilities are essential for modern CIAM solutions, enabling businesses to connect identity services with third-party applications and digital ecosystems. Many businesses rely on external partners, payment gateways, and e-commerce platforms to deliver a seamless customer experience. CIAM platforms use secure APIs and authentication protocols to facilitate integration while maintaining data security. API gateways and access control mechanisms ensure that customer identities remain protected even when interacting with external services.

Logging, monitoring, and analytics play a vital role in maintaining security and compliance in CIAM solutions. Businesses need visibility into authentication events, failed login attempts, and access patterns to detect potential security threats and optimize user experiences. CIAM platforms provide real-time monitoring dashboards, audit logs, and reporting tools that help organizations track user activities and generate compliance reports. Advanced analytics capabilities allow businesses to identify trends, improve authentication workflows, and enhance security posture based on data-driven insights.

Customer lifecycle management ensures that identity data remains accurate and secure throughout the customer's relationship with a business. CIAM solutions manage identity creation, profile updates, and account deactivation based on user activity and business rules. Automated lifecycle management processes help businesses maintain data hygiene, reduce security risks associated with inactive accounts, and comply with regulatory requirements for data retention and deletion.

By incorporating these core components, CIAM solutions enable businesses to provide secure, scalable, and seamless digital experiences while ensuring regulatory compliance and customer trust. A well-implemented CIAM strategy not only enhances security but also improves user engagement, driving long-term business success in an increasingly digital world.

Authentication Methods in CIAM

Authentication is the foundation of Customer Identity and Access Management (CIAM), ensuring that users can securely access digital services while protecting sensitive information. The right authentication method balances security and convenience, reducing friction for legitimate users while preventing unauthorized access. As cyber threats evolve, businesses must adopt authentication strategies that go beyond traditional username and password combinations. CIAM solutions provide a variety of authentication methods to accommodate different user preferences, security requirements, and regulatory standards.

Password-based authentication remains one of the most widely used methods despite its vulnerabilities. Users create a unique password during registration and enter it each time they log in. While this method is simple, it poses significant security risks, including password reuse, weak passwords, and susceptibility to phishing attacks. Many users struggle to remember complex passwords, leading them to choose weak credentials or reuse them across multiple accounts. To mitigate these risks, CIAM platforms enforce password policies that require minimum complexity, expiration periods, and restrictions on commonly used passwords. However, businesses increasingly look for alternative authentication methods to reduce reliance on passwords and improve security.

Multi-factor authentication (MFA) enhances security by requiring users to verify their identity using two or more factors. These factors fall into three categories: something the user knows (password or PIN), something the user has (mobile device or security token), and something the user is (biometric data such as fingerprint or facial recognition). MFA significantly reduces the risk of unauthorized access, as even if one factor is compromised, an attacker would still need to bypass additional security measures. Businesses implement MFA through methods such as SMS-based one-time passcodes (OTPs), authenticator apps, hardware security keys, and biometric verification. While MFA adds an extra step to the authentication process, it is one of the most effective ways to prevent credential-based attacks.

Passwordless authentication eliminates the need for traditional passwords, offering a more secure and user-friendly alternative. Users authenticate using methods such as email-based magic links, biometric verification, or authentication apps that generate one-time codes. Magic links allow users to receive a temporary login link via email, bypassing the need for a password entirely. Biometric authentication uses facial recognition, fingerprints, or voice recognition to verify identity, making it highly secure and convenient. Many modern CIAM solutions integrate with biometric authentication options available on smartphones and other devices. Passwordless authentication improves security by reducing phishing risks, eliminating weak passwords, and streamlining the login experience.

Social login simplifies authentication by allowing users to log in using their existing credentials from third-party providers such as Google, Facebook, Apple, or LinkedIn. Instead of creating a new username and password, users authenticate through their preferred social account, reducing registration friction and improving convenience. Social login benefits businesses by speeding up onboarding, increasing conversion rates, and ensuring that user accounts are linked to verified identities. However, it also requires careful consideration of data privacy and consent management, as businesses must comply with regulations when collecting user information from third-party platforms.

Single Sign-On (SSO) enables users to log in once and gain access to multiple services without re-entering credentials. This authentication method improves user experience by reducing the need for multiple passwords while enhancing security through centralized authentication controls. Businesses that operate multiple brands or services within the same ecosystem benefit from SSO by providing a seamless experience across platforms. CIAM solutions support SSO using authentication protocols such as Security Assertion Markup Language (SAML) and OpenID Connect (OIDC), ensuring secure interoperability between different applications.

Risk-based authentication dynamically adjusts security requirements based on contextual factors such as location, device, login behavior, and past activity. If a user logs in from a familiar device and location, the authentication process may proceed with minimal friction. However, if a login attempt originates from an unusual location or a device never used before, the system may prompt additional verification steps, such as MFA. Risk-based authentication improves security without compromising user experience by applying stricter security measures only when necessary. CIAM platforms leverage artificial intelligence and machine learning to analyze user behavior in real-time, detecting anomalies and potential threats before they escalate.

Device authentication associates a user's identity with a trusted device, allowing seamless and secure access without repeated authentication prompts. This method is commonly used in mobile apps, where users authenticate once and remain logged in unless they switch devices or reset credentials. CIAM solutions use techniques such as device fingerprinting, secure tokens, and certificate-based authentication to verify the legitimacy of a device. Businesses benefit from device authentication by enhancing security while minimizing login disruptions for returning users.

Federated authentication allows users to access multiple services using a single identity managed by an identity provider (IdP). Instead of creating separate accounts for different platforms, users authenticate through an external provider that issues secure authentication tokens. CIAM solutions support federated authentication using standards such as OAuth 2.0, OpenID Connect, and SAML, enabling seamless integration between different digital ecosystems. Federated authentication is especially beneficial for businesses operating partner networks, multi-brand platforms, or B2B environments where customers need access to multiple services with a single login.

Time-based one-time passwords (TOTP) provide a secure authentication method that generates temporary passcodes valid for a short period. TOTP authentication is commonly used in combination with MFA, where users enter a one-time code generated by an authenticator app such as Google Authenticator or Microsoft Authenticator. Unlike SMS-based OTPs, which are vulnerable to interception, TOTP codes are generated locally on the user's device, making them more secure. Businesses that require strong authentication without relying on SMS verification often implement TOTP to enhance security while ensuring ease of use.

Push notification authentication streamlines the login process by allowing users to approve authentication requests through a mobile app. Instead of entering a password or OTP, users receive a push notification prompting them to confirm or deny the login attempt. This method reduces reliance on passwords while providing a highly secure and frictionless experience. Businesses that prioritize user convenience adopt push notification authentication as a modern alternative to traditional MFA methods.

QR code authentication is an emerging authentication method that enables users to log in by scanning a QR code using their mobile device. This method is particularly useful for passwordless authentication, where users scan the code displayed on a website or kiosk to verify their identity. QR code authentication enhances security by eliminating the need for passwords while offering a fast and user-friendly authentication experience. Businesses leveraging mobile-first strategies integrate QR code authentication to provide a seamless and secure login process.

By combining multiple authentication methods, businesses can create a flexible and secure CIAM strategy tailored to their customers' needs. CIAM platforms allow organizations to implement adaptive authentication policies, ensuring that the right level of security is applied based on user risk profiles and business requirements. Authentication is no longer just about verifying identity; it is about delivering a seamless, secure, and personalized experience that meets the evolving expectations of digital users.

Single Sign-On (SSO) for Customer Identities

Single Sign-On (SSO) is a critical feature in Customer Identity and Access Management (CIAM) that enhances both security and user experience by allowing customers to access multiple applications with a single set of credentials. In a digital environment where users interact with numerous services, SSO eliminates the need to remember multiple usernames and passwords, reducing friction and improving convenience. Businesses that implement SSO effectively provide a seamless authentication experience while maintaining strong security and compliance.

The traditional authentication model requires users to create separate login credentials for each application they access. This approach often leads to frustration, password fatigue, and increased security risks due to password reuse. SSO simplifies the authentication process by enabling users to log in once and gain access to multiple applications within the same ecosystem. Instead of requiring users to re-enter credentials for every service, SSO authenticates them once and manages session continuity across different platforms. This approach improves usability while reducing the likelihood of forgotten passwords and account lockouts.

Security is a major concern in digital identity management, and SSO plays a key role in strengthening security while minimizing vulnerabilities. When users are required to manage multiple passwords, they often resort to weak or easily guessable credentials.

SSO eliminates the need for multiple passwords, reducing the attack surface for cybercriminals who exploit poor password hygiene. By centralizing authentication, businesses can enforce stronger security policies, including multi-factor authentication (MFA) and risk-based authentication, without adding complexity for users. If a security threat is detected in one session, businesses can immediately revoke access across all connected services, reducing the risk of unauthorized access.

User experience is a critical factor in customer engagement, and SSO significantly enhances usability. Customers expect instant access to digital services without unnecessary authentication barriers. When a business operates multiple websites, applications, or services, requiring users to log in separately for each one creates frustration and may lead to abandonment. SSO eliminates redundant login processes, allowing customers to move seamlessly between different services without interruption. This streamlined experience increases customer satisfaction and loyalty by providing a consistent and effortless authentication journey.

Scalability is another important advantage of SSO in CIAM. Businesses that serve large user bases across multiple digital platforms need an authentication solution that can handle high volumes of login requests without compromising performance. SSO enables organizations to manage authentication efficiently while reducing infrastructure complexity. Cloud-based CIAM solutions with SSO capabilities provide elastic scalability, ensuring that authentication processes remain fast and reliable even during peak usage periods. Whether a business is onboarding new users, expanding into new markets, or integrating with third-party services, SSO offers the flexibility to scale authentication operations seamlessly.

Compliance with data privacy regulations is an essential consideration in identity management, and SSO helps businesses meet regulatory requirements. Laws such as the General Data Protection Regulation (GDPR) and the California Consumer Privacy Act (CCPA) mandate that organizations protect user credentials and manage customer data responsibly. SSO centralizes identity management, allowing businesses to implement consistent security controls and access policies. By reducing the number of authentication points, SSO minimizes the exposure of credentials, decreasing the risk of data breaches and unauthorized access. Additionally, businesses can provide users with clear visibility and control over their authentication sessions, ensuring compliance with transparency and data protection requirements.

Federated identity is closely linked to SSO, enabling users to authenticate across multiple organizations or service providers using a single identity. Standards such as OAuth 2.0, OpenID Connect (OIDC), and Security Assertion Markup Language (SAML) facilitate secure authentication across different platforms. Businesses that integrate SSO with federated identity management can offer seamless authentication experiences while maintaining security and interoperability. For example, a user who logs into a social media platform can use the same credentials to access partner services without creating new accounts. This integration reduces friction, accelerates onboarding, and enhances user convenience while ensuring secure authentication.

Cross-device authentication is another benefit of SSO in CIAM. Customers frequently switch between desktops, mobile devices, tablets, and IoT-enabled applications. SSO ensures that users remain authenticated across multiple devices without the need for repeated logins. Whether a customer starts a transaction on a smartphone and completes it on a laptop or accesses services through a smart TV, SSO maintains session continuity, providing a frictionless digital experience. Businesses that prioritize cross-device authentication improve customer retention and engagement by offering uninterrupted access to their services.

API security is a crucial aspect of SSO implementation in CIAM. Many businesses rely on APIs to connect applications, integrate third-party services, and facilitate data exchange. SSO solutions use secure authentication protocols to protect API access and ensure that only authorized users can interact with digital services. Token-based authentication mechanisms, such as JSON Web Tokens (JWT), enable secure session management and minimize the risk of credential exposure. By implementing SSO with API security best practices, businesses protect customer identities while enabling seamless integration between different digital services.

Fraud prevention and risk-based authentication enhance the effectiveness of SSO in CIAM. Businesses must ensure that a compromised session in one application does not lead to unauthorized access across multiple services. Risk-based authentication analyzes contextual factors such as login behavior, location, device, and transaction history to detect anomalies and potential threats. If suspicious activity is identified, the system can require additional verification steps or terminate the session altogether. This proactive approach prevents account takeovers and fraudulent transactions while maintaining a seamless authentication experience for legitimate users.

Self-service account management is another advantage of SSO in customer identity management. Customers should have the ability to manage their authentication preferences, review active sessions, and revoke access when necessary. CIAM platforms with SSO capabilities provide user-friendly dashboards where customers can control their authentication settings, manage connected accounts, and receive security notifications. Empowering users with self-service options enhances transparency and trust while reducing support requests related to login issues and password resets.

Businesses that implement SSO as part of their CIAM strategy gain a competitive advantage by delivering secure, scalable, and user-friendly authentication experiences. By simplifying login processes, strengthening security, and ensuring compliance, SSO enhances customer engagement while reducing operational complexities. Organizations that operate across multiple digital platforms benefit from SSO's ability to streamline authentication and create a cohesive user journey. As digital interactions continue to expand, SSO will remain a key enabler of seamless identity management and secure access for customers worldwide.

Multi-Factor Authentication (MFA) Strategies

Multi-Factor Authentication (MFA) is a fundamental security measure in Customer Identity and Access Management (CIAM) that enhances protection by requiring users to verify their identity using multiple authentication factors. As cyber threats become more sophisticated, businesses must implement MFA strategies to safeguard customer accounts, prevent unauthorized access, and reduce fraud risks. By incorporating MFA into their authentication processes, organizations balance security and user experience, ensuring that customers can access digital services safely without unnecessary friction.

MFA relies on the principle of requiring at least two or more factors from different categories: something the user knows, something the user has, and something the user is. The most common implementation combines a traditional password with an additional verification step, such as a one-time password (OTP) sent via SMS or email. However, modern MFA strategies go beyond basic two-factor authentication (2FA) to incorporate more advanced and seamless authentication methods that improve both security and usability.

One of the most widely used MFA methods is SMS-based OTP authentication. In this approach, users receive a one-time passcode via SMS, which they must enter after providing their primary credentials. While SMS-based authentication is easy to implement and familiar to most users, it has security vulnerabilities, including SIM swapping attacks and interception risks. Cybercriminals can exploit weaknesses in mobile networks to gain unauthorized access to OTPs, making SMS-based authentication less reliable for high-security applications. Businesses looking for stronger MFA strategies often explore alternatives to SMS authentication to mitigate these risks.

Authenticator apps provide a more secure alternative to SMS-based MFA. Applications such as Google Authenticator, Microsoft Authenticator, and Authy generate time-based one-time passwords (TOTP) that refresh every 30 to 60 seconds. Since these codes are generated locally on the user's device and do not rely on SMS delivery, they are less susceptible to interception and fraud. Authenticator apps improve security while offering a convenient authentication experience, making them a preferred option for many organizations implementing MFA in their CIAM frameworks.

Push notification authentication is another effective MFA strategy that enhances both security and usability. Instead of entering an OTP manually, users receive a push notification on their mobile device prompting them to approve or deny the authentication request. This method simplifies the authentication process by allowing users to verify their identity with a single tap. Push notifications also incorporate contextual information, such as device details and login location, helping users detect suspicious login attempts. Businesses adopting push authentication benefit from reduced friction, faster login times, and increased protection against phishing attacks.

Biometric authentication is becoming a key component of MFA strategies in CIAM. Fingerprint recognition, facial recognition, and voice authentication provide a high level of security while eliminating the need for passwords and OTPs. Biometrics leverage unique physical characteristics that are difficult to replicate, making them highly effective for preventing unauthorized access. Modern smartphones and laptops come equipped with biometric sensors, enabling seamless authentication experiences for users. Businesses integrating biometrics into their MFA strategies enhance security while delivering a frictionless login process for customers.

Hardware security keys offer one of the most robust MFA options available. These physical devices, such as YubiKeys and Google Titan Security Keys, use cryptographic authentication to verify user identity. When logging in, users insert the hardware key into a USB port or tap it against a compatible NFC-enabled device to complete the authentication process. Unlike OTPs or SMS-based MFA, hardware security keys are resistant to phishing and remote attacks, providing an additional layer of protection for high-value transactions and sensitive accounts. Businesses that require maximum security often implement hardware-based MFA to safeguard customer identities against sophisticated cyber threats.

Risk-based authentication (RBA) enhances MFA by dynamically adjusting authentication requirements based on real-time risk analysis.

Instead of applying the same authentication steps to every login attempt, RBA evaluates factors such as device reputation, geographic location, behavioral patterns, and login history to determine the appropriate level of authentication. If a user logs in from a trusted device and familiar location, the system may allow access with minimal friction. However, if the login attempt originates from an unfamiliar location or suspicious IP address, the system may trigger additional verification steps, such as MFA prompts or biometric authentication. RBA helps businesses maintain security while optimizing user experience by reducing unnecessary authentication challenges for low-risk users.

Adaptive authentication takes risk-based authentication a step further by continuously analyzing user behavior and adapting security measures accordingly. AI-driven CIAM solutions monitor login trends, account activity, and transaction patterns to detect anomalies and potential threats. If unusual behavior is detected, adaptive authentication can escalate security requirements in real time, prompting users to verify their identity using MFA. This approach ensures that legitimate users can access their accounts smoothly while preventing fraudsters from exploiting stolen credentials. Businesses implementing adaptive authentication strengthen their security posture while maintaining a seamless experience for customers.

Passwordless authentication is an emerging MFA strategy that eliminates the need for passwords altogether. Instead of requiring users to remember complex passwords, passwordless authentication relies on more secure alternatives such as biometric verification, magic links, and cryptographic keys. Users receive a unique authentication link via email or mobile app, allowing them to log in with a single click. This method enhances security by reducing the risks associated with password reuse, credential stuffing, and phishing attacks. As more organizations move toward passwordless authentication, CIAM solutions are evolving to support these methods within their MFA frameworks.

MFA implementation must also consider user convenience and accessibility. While stronger authentication methods improve security, excessive authentication prompts can lead to frustration and abandonment. Businesses must strike a balance by offering multiple authentication options and allowing users to choose the method that best suits their needs. A customer logging in from a secure, familiar device should not be forced to complete multiple MFA steps unnecessarily. CIAM platforms that offer flexible authentication policies and intelligent risk assessments improve adoption rates and overall user satisfaction.

Businesses adopting MFA in their CIAM strategies must also ensure compliance with industry regulations and data protection standards. Regulatory requirements such as the General Data Protection Regulation (GDPR) and the Payment Services Directive (PSD2) mandate strong customer authentication for certain transactions. By implementing MFA, organizations meet compliance obligations while protecting customer data from unauthorized access. Secure authentication practices help businesses build trust with their customers and demonstrate a commitment to privacy and security.

A successful MFA strategy requires continuous monitoring and improvement. Cyber threats evolve rapidly, and authentication methods must adapt to counter new attack vectors. Businesses should regularly review authentication logs, analyze security trends, and update MFA policies based on emerging threats. CIAM platforms with built-in analytics and reporting tools provide valuable insights into authentication performance, helping organizations optimize security while maintaining a frictionless user experience.

Multi-Factor Authentication is a critical component of modern CIAM solutions, offering enhanced security while enabling seamless customer interactions. By leveraging a combination of authentication methods, businesses create a robust identity protection framework that safeguards customer accounts from cyber threats. A well-executed MFA strategy not only reduces fraud risks but also improves user trust and engagement, making it an essential part of digital identity management.

Open Standards in CIAM: OAuth, OIDC, and SAML

Customer Identity and Access Management (CIAM) relies on open standards to provide secure, interoperable, and scalable authentication and authorization mechanisms. Among the most widely used standards in modern CIAM implementations are OAuth 2.0, OpenID Connect (OIDC), and Security Assertion Markup Language (SAML). These protocols facilitate secure identity management by enabling users to authenticate across multiple applications and services without exposing sensitive credentials. By leveraging these standards, organizations can improve security, enhance user experience, and ensure compliance with industry regulations.

OAuth 2.0 is a widely adopted authorization framework that allows users to grant third-party applications limited access to their resources without sharing their login credentials. Instead of requiring users to provide their usernames and passwords directly to third-party applications, OAuth 2.0 issues access tokens that authorize applications to interact with user accounts securely. These tokens have expiration times and can be revoked if necessary, reducing the risk of credential theft and unauthorized access. OAuth 2.0 operates through different grant types, such as authorization code, implicit, resource owner password credentials, and client credentials, each designed for specific use cases.

The authorization code grant is the most commonly used OAuth 2.0 flow for web and mobile applications. It involves redirecting users to an authorization server, where they authenticate and grant permissions to the requesting application. Once authorized, the application receives an authorization code, which it exchanges for an access token. This method provides an added layer of security, as the authorization code is transmitted separately from user credentials, reducing the risk of interception. The implicit grant, which was once used in browser-based applications, has largely been deprecated in favor of more secure alternatives. The resource owner password credentials grant allows users to provide their credentials directly to an application, making it suitable for highly trusted applications but less secure for general use. The client credentials grant is typically used for machine-to-machine communication, where no user interaction is required.

While OAuth 2.0 is designed for authorization, OpenID Connect (OIDC) extends it to include authentication. OIDC is an identity layer built on top of OAuth 2.0 that enables applications to verify user identities and obtain basic profile information. By introducing an ID token in addition to the access token, OIDC allows applications to confirm that a user has authenticated with an identity provider. This makes it possible to implement single sign-on (SSO) solutions, where users authenticate once and gain access to multiple applications without needing to log in repeatedly.

OIDC simplifies authentication by using a standard set of endpoints, including the authorization endpoint, token endpoint, and user info endpoint. The authorization endpoint is where users authenticate and authorize access, while the token endpoint issues access and ID tokens. The user info endpoint allows applications to retrieve additional details about the authenticated user, such as their name, email, and profile picture. These standardized endpoints ensure interoperability between different identity providers and applications, making OIDC an essential component of modern CIAM strategies.

Security Assertion Markup Language (SAML) is another open standard used for authentication and authorization, primarily in enterprise environments. Unlike OAuth 2.0 and OIDC, which are based on JSON and RESTful APIs, SAML relies on XML-based assertions to exchange authentication and authorization data between identity providers and service providers. SAML enables SSO by allowing users to authenticate once with an identity provider and access multiple applications without needing to log in again. This is particularly useful in corporate environments where employees need seamless access to various enterprise applications.

A SAML authentication flow involves three key entities: the user, the identity provider, and the service provider. When a user attempts to access a service provider's application, they are redirected to the identity provider for authentication. Once authenticated, the identity provider generates a SAML assertion containing user attributes and authentication details, which is then sent to the service provider. The service provider validates the assertion and grants access to the user. SAML supports both identity provider-initiated and service provider-initiated authentication flows, providing flexibility in how authentication requests are handled.

Despite its widespread use in enterprise environments, SAML is gradually being replaced by OIDC in consumer-facing applications due to its complexity and reliance on XML. However, many organizations still use SAML for federated authentication in corporate networks, government agencies, and higher education institutions. Integrating SAML with OIDC-based CIAM solutions allows businesses to support legacy authentication mechanisms while transitioning to modern identity standards.

Each of these open standards plays a distinct role in CIAM, and many organizations use a combination of OAuth 2.0, OIDC, and SAML to meet their authentication and authorization requirements. OAuth 2.0 provides a secure way to grant third-party access to user resources, OIDC enables seamless authentication and SSO, and SAML facilitates identity federation in enterprise environments. By adopting these standards, businesses can create flexible and secure identity management systems that enhance user experience while mitigating security risks.

The future of CIAM will continue to be shaped by advancements in these standards, with ongoing efforts to enhance security and interoperability. OAuth 2.1, an upcoming update to OAuth 2.0, aims to simplify the framework by removing deprecated features and improving security best practices. OIDC will continue to evolve with stronger support for decentralized identity and verifiable credentials, enabling users to maintain greater control over their digital identities. Meanwhile, SAML remains relevant in enterprise identity federation, with organizations gradually integrating it with modern authentication protocols.

As businesses expand their digital ecosystems, implementing open standards in CIAM is essential for ensuring secure, scalable, and user-friendly authentication experiences. By leveraging OAuth 2.0, OIDC, and SAML, organizations can protect user identities, reduce authentication friction, and support seamless cross-platform access. These standards not only enhance security but also foster trust and interoperability, allowing businesses to provide secure digital services while maintaining compliance with industry regulations.

Passwordless Authentication in CIAM

Passwordless authentication is transforming the way businesses manage customer identities by eliminating the reliance on traditional passwords. In Customer Identity and Access Management (CIAM), passwordless authentication provides a more secure and user-friendly experience by leveraging alternative methods such as biometrics, magic links, one-time passcodes (OTPs), and hardware security keys. This approach enhances security, reduces friction, and minimizes the risks associated with password-based authentication, such as credential theft, phishing attacks, and password fatigue.

The traditional username and password model has long been a source of frustration for users and security teams alike. Customers often struggle to remember complex passwords, leading them to reuse weak credentials across multiple accounts. This behavior increases the likelihood of credential stuffing attacks, where hackers exploit leaked passwords to gain unauthorized access to accounts. Businesses that rely on password-based authentication face significant security challenges, including frequent account recovery requests, phishing attacks, and data breaches. Passwordless authentication addresses these issues by replacing passwords with more secure and convenient authentication methods.

One of the most widely adopted forms of passwordless authentication is biometric authentication. This method verifies a user's identity using unique physical characteristics such as fingerprints, facial recognition, or voice patterns. Smartphones, laptops, and other smart devices now come equipped with biometric sensors, making biometric authentication both accessible and highly secure. Unlike passwords, biometric data cannot be easily stolen or guessed, providing a strong layer of protection against unauthorized access. In CIAM, biometric authentication enhances user experience by allowing customers to log in instantly without the need to remember or enter credentials.

Magic links offer another effective passwordless authentication method. When a user attempts to log in, they receive an email containing a unique, time-sensitive link. Clicking on the link grants them access to their account without requiring a password. Magic links eliminate the need for users to remember complex credentials while ensuring that only authorized users with access to their registered email accounts can authenticate successfully. Businesses implementing magic links in their CIAM strategy benefit from reduced login friction and fewer support requests related to forgotten passwords.

One-time passcodes (OTPs) are commonly used as a passwordless authentication method in CIAM. Instead of relying on static passwords, users receive a unique, temporary code via SMS, email, or an authenticator app. These passcodes expire after a short period, preventing attackers from reusing stolen credentials. OTPs improve security by ensuring that authentication relies on a fresh, dynamically generated code each time a user logs in. However, businesses must consider the security risks associated with SMS-based OTPs, such as SIM swapping attacks and interception vulnerabilities. Using authenticator apps or email-based OTPs provides a more secure alternative.

Hardware security keys, such as YubiKeys or Google Titan Security Keys, provide a highly secure passwordless authentication option. These physical devices use cryptographic authentication to verify a user's identity when inserted into a USB port or tapped against an NFC-enabled device. Hardware security keys are resistant to phishing attacks, as they do not transmit static credentials that can be intercepted or reused. In CIAM, businesses that require high-security authentication, such as financial services or enterprise applications, implement hardware keys to protect customer accounts from unauthorized access.

Push notification authentication is another passwordless method that simplifies user verification. When a customer attempts to log in, they receive a push notification on their mobile device asking them to approve or deny the authentication request. This method reduces friction by allowing users to authenticate with a single tap, while also incorporating contextual security checks such as device information, location, and IP address. Push authentication enhances security by requiring physical device interaction, making it resistant to credential-based attacks.

QR code authentication provides a seamless and secure passwordless login experience. Instead of entering credentials, users scan a QR code displayed on a website using their mobile device. The mobile app verifies the user's identity and grants access without requiring a password. This method is particularly useful for businesses with mobile-first users or those looking to streamline authentication across multiple devices. QR code authentication eliminates password-related risks while offering a quick and convenient login experience.

The adoption of passwordless authentication in CIAM is driven by the need to improve security while enhancing user experience. Businesses that transition to passwordless authentication reduce operational costs associated with password management, such as help desk support for password resets and account recovery. Additionally, removing passwords as an authentication factor significantly reduces the risk of phishing attacks, brute force attacks, and unauthorized access due to credential leaks.

Passwordless authentication also aligns with modern security frameworks such as Zero Trust, where continuous verification is required before granting access. By leveraging strong authentication methods, businesses ensure that user identities are verified based on secure, context-aware factors rather than static passwords. This proactive approach strengthens security while enabling seamless access across digital services.

Implementing passwordless authentication in CIAM requires careful planning and user education. Businesses must ensure that users are comfortable with new authentication methods and provide clear instructions on how to transition from password-based logins. Offering multiple passwordless options allows users to choose the method that best suits their needs, improving adoption rates and minimizing resistance to change.

Regulatory compliance is another consideration when implementing passwordless authentication. Data protection laws such as the General Data Protection Regulation (GDPR) and the California Consumer Privacy Act (CCPA) require businesses to implement secure authentication measures to protect customer identities. Passwordless authentication supports compliance by reducing exposure to credential theft and providing stronger authentication mechanisms that align with regulatory security standards.

CIAM platforms that support passwordless authentication integrate with existing identity providers, applications, and security frameworks to ensure seamless authentication experiences. Businesses adopting passwordless authentication benefit from enhanced security, improved user satisfaction, and reduced reliance on outdated password-based security models. As digital threats continue to evolve, passwordless authentication is emerging as a critical component of modern identity management, providing a secure, scalable, and user-friendly authentication solution for businesses and their customers.

Social Login and Third-Party Authentication

Social login and third-party authentication have become essential features in modern Customer Identity and Access Management (CIAM) solutions, allowing users to authenticate using their existing accounts from external providers such as Google, Facebook, Apple, LinkedIn, and Microsoft. This approach simplifies the registration and login process, reduces friction for users, and enhances security by leveraging trusted identity providers. Businesses that implement social login and third-party authentication benefit from improved user experience, increased conversion rates, and reduced password-related security risks.

The traditional method of creating and managing accounts with unique usernames and passwords has become increasingly burdensome for users. Remembering multiple credentials across different services often leads to password fatigue, forcing users to resort to weak passwords, reuse credentials, or abandon account creation altogether. Social login eliminates this problem by allowing users to authenticate with credentials they already trust and use regularly. Instead of requiring a new password, users can log in with a single click, leveraging their existing social media or third-party accounts. This streamlined process enhances customer experience by making authentication effortless and reducing barriers to account creation.

From a business perspective, social login accelerates user onboarding and reduces drop-off rates during registration. Many potential customers abandon sign-up forms when they are too lengthy or require extensive information. Social login simplifies this process by pre-filling basic profile details such as name, email address, and profile picture, eliminating the need for users to manually enter this information. Faster onboarding means higher conversion rates, increased engagement, and a better overall user experience.

Security is another key advantage of social login and third-party authentication. By leveraging external identity providers, businesses can offload authentication security to established platforms that already implement advanced security measures such as multi-factor authentication (MFA), biometric verification, and continuous risk assessment. Social login reduces the risk of credential stuffing, brute-force attacks, and phishing attempts since users do not need to create or store additional passwords. When implemented correctly, social login enhances security while maintaining convenience for users.

Another important benefit of social login is the ability to improve personalization and customer engagement. When users authenticate through a social identity provider, businesses gain access to verified identity attributes such as name, location, language preferences, and profile interests. This information allows organizations to tailor content, recommend personalized products, and create a more engaging user experience. Social login also enables businesses to track user activity across different touchpoints, providing valuable insights that drive marketing strategies and customer retention efforts.

Despite its advantages, businesses must consider the privacy and regulatory implications of social login and third-party authentication. Users are becoming increasingly aware of how their data is shared and used, and businesses must ensure compliance with data protection laws such as the General Data Protection Regulation (GDPR) and the California Consumer Privacy Act (CCPA). Transparent consent management is crucial, allowing users to control what information they share and how it is used. CIAM solutions must provide clear privacy policies, consent forms, and opt-out mechanisms to maintain user trust and compliance with legal requirements.

Third-party authentication extends beyond social login by enabling users to authenticate through enterprise identity providers, government-issued digital identities, or industry-specific federated identity networks. Businesses operating in regulated sectors such as finance, healthcare, and education may integrate with trusted third-party identity verification services to ensure secure and compliant authentication. For example, a financial institution may authenticate users through an external banking identity provider, verifying customer credentials before granting access to sensitive financial transactions.

The technical implementation of social login and third-party authentication requires integrating with authentication protocols such as OAuth 2.0, OpenID Connect (OIDC), and Security Assertion Markup Language (SAML). OAuth 2.0 enables secure authorization without exposing user credentials, allowing businesses to request specific scopes of access to user data while ensuring security. OpenID Connect extends OAuth 2.0 by providing authentication capabilities, enabling businesses to verify a user's identity and retrieve identity attributes. SAML is often used in enterprise environments to support single sign-on (SSO) across multiple organizations and identity providers.

Businesses must also consider potential risks associated with social login and third-party authentication. While external identity providers enhance security, they introduce dependencies on third-party services. If a social identity provider experiences an outage, users may be unable to authenticate, impacting business operations. To mitigate this risk, organizations should implement fallback authentication mechanisms such as email-based login or alternative identity providers. Additionally, businesses must regularly monitor third-party authentication integrations to ensure compatibility, security updates, and compliance with changing regulations.

Another consideration is the potential for user lockout if a third-party account is compromised or deactivated. For example, if a customer's social media account is suspended or deleted, they may lose access to services that rely on social login. To prevent account loss, businesses should provide users with backup authentication options, such as linking multiple identity providers, enabling passwordless authentication, or allowing users to recover accounts through verified email or phone numbers.

Businesses implementing social login and third-party authentication must balance convenience with security and privacy. Offering multiple authentication options ensures inclusivity for users who may not want to use social login due to privacy concerns or lack of access to certain providers. Providing transparent consent management, secure data handling, and backup authentication options builds trust and ensures a positive user experience.

As digital interactions continue to evolve, social login and third-party authentication play an increasingly important role in CIAM strategies. Businesses that leverage these authentication methods effectively can enhance user experience, strengthen security, and streamline access across digital ecosystems. By integrating with trusted identity providers, organizations can reduce authentication friction, improve customer engagement, and provide a seamless and secure authentication experience for users worldwide.

Identity Federation and CIAM

Identity federation is a key concept in Customer Identity and Access Management (CIAM) that enables users to access multiple services using a single set of credentials from a trusted identity provider. By establishing trust relationships between different organizations, applications, and platforms, identity federation simplifies authentication, enhances security, and improves user experience. In an increasingly interconnected digital world, businesses must implement identity federation strategies to support seamless authentication across various digital ecosystems while maintaining strong security controls.

Traditional authentication methods require users to create separate accounts and manage different passwords for each service they access. This approach often leads to password fatigue, increased security risks, and poor user experience. Identity federation eliminates the need for multiple credentials by allowing users to authenticate once and gain access to multiple services without re-entering credentials. Instead of storing and managing user credentials in each application, businesses can rely on a central identity provider to handle authentication and authorization.

Federated identity management is based on trust relationships between identity providers (IdPs) and service providers (SPs). The identity provider is responsible for verifying user identities and issuing authentication tokens that allow users to access various applications and services. Service providers rely on these tokens to grant access without requiring users to reauthenticate. This approach reduces administrative overhead, improves security, and streamlines the authentication process across multiple domains.

Several industry-standard authentication protocols enable identity federation in CIAM, including Security Assertion Markup Language (SAML), OpenID Connect (OIDC), and OAuth 2.0. SAML is widely used in enterprise environments and government sectors to enable Single Sign-On (SSO) across multiple applications. OpenID Connect extends OAuth 2.0 by providing authentication capabilities, allowing businesses to verify user identities and retrieve identity attributes from a trusted provider. OAuth 2.0 is commonly used for API security, enabling secure authorization between different digital services.

One of the primary benefits of identity federation is Single Sign-On (SSO), which allows users to authenticate once and gain access to multiple applications without repeated logins. SSO improves user convenience by reducing authentication friction while enhancing security through centralized identity management. Businesses that implement federated SSO enable customers to move seamlessly between different digital properties without the need for multiple login credentials. This approach is particularly valuable for organizations that operate multiple brands, partner networks, or industry collaborations where users need access to various services.

Identity federation also enhances security by reducing the risk of credential-based attacks such as phishing, credential stuffing, and password reuse. Since users do not need to create and store separate passwords for each service, the attack surface for cybercriminals is significantly reduced. Federated authentication relies on strong identity verification mechanisms, including multi-factor authentication (MFA) and risk-based authentication, to ensure that only legitimate users gain access to protected resources. By centralizing identity verification, businesses can enforce consistent security policies and respond quickly to security threats.

Another advantage of identity federation is improved compliance with data protection regulations such as the General Data Protection Regulation (GDPR) and the California Consumer Privacy Act (CCPA). These regulations require businesses to implement secure authentication mechanisms, protect user credentials, and provide transparency in data handling practices. By leveraging identity federation, businesses can reduce the need to store and manage user credentials, minimizing the risk of data breaches and ensuring compliance with regulatory requirements. Additionally, federated authentication enables users to control their privacy settings and manage consent preferences more effectively.

Cross-industry identity federation is becoming increasingly important as businesses collaborate across different sectors. Financial institutions, healthcare providers, government agencies, and technology companies are adopting federated identity frameworks to enable secure and seamless authentication across their digital ecosystems. For example, banks may integrate with third-party financial services through identity federation, allowing customers to authenticate using their banking credentials without exposing their passwords to external platforms. Similarly, healthcare providers can enable secure access to patient records across different institutions while maintaining strict privacy controls.

Interoperability is a critical consideration in identity federation. Businesses must ensure that their CIAM solutions support multiple authentication protocols and integrate with various identity providers to enable seamless authentication experiences. Open standards such as SAML, OIDC, and OAuth 2.0 facilitate interoperability by enabling different systems to communicate securely and exchange identity information. Organizations that adopt flexible CIAM solutions with strong identity federation capabilities can integrate with third-party services, cloud applications, and partner networks without compromising security or user experience.

Businesses implementing identity federation must also address potential challenges, including identity provider selection, trust management, and user account linking. Selecting the right identity provider is crucial, as it determines the level of security, scalability, and reliability of federated authentication. Organizations must establish trust policies, enforce security standards, and monitor authentication events to prevent unauthorized access. Additionally, businesses need to provide seamless account linking mechanisms to ensure that existing user accounts are properly associated with federated identities.

User experience plays a significant role in the success of identity federation. While federated authentication simplifies access, businesses must ensure that users understand how their identities are managed and provide clear instructions on authentication processes. Providing self-service options for account recovery, identity linking, and consent management enhances user trust and engagement. Customers should have the ability to manage their authentication preferences, review connected accounts, and revoke access to third-party services when necessary.

The adoption of decentralized identity models is an emerging trend in identity federation. Decentralized identity shifts control of digital identities from centralized identity providers to individual users, allowing them to manage their credentials using blockchain-based identity wallets. This approach enhances privacy, reduces reliance on third-party identity providers, and gives users greater control over their digital identities. While decentralized identity is still in its early stages, it has the potential to transform identity federation by enabling self-sovereign identity management and reducing dependency on traditional authentication providers.

Identity federation is a critical component of modern CIAM strategies, enabling businesses to provide seamless, secure, and scalable authentication experiences across digital ecosystems. By leveraging federated authentication, organizations enhance security, improve user experience, and ensure compliance with data protection regulations. As digital interactions continue to evolve, identity federation will play a central role in enabling secure and frictionless authentication across interconnected platforms and industries.

Customer Identity Lifecycle Management

Customer Identity Lifecycle Management is a critical aspect of Customer Identity and Access Management (CIAM) that governs the entire journey of a customer's identity within an organization's digital ecosystem. From initial registration to eventual account deletion, businesses must implement secure, efficient, and compliant identity management processes to ensure a seamless user experience while maintaining security and regulatory adherence. Managing customer identities throughout their lifecycle involves various stages, including onboarding, authentication, authorization, profile management, consent handling, activity monitoring, and secure deprovisioning.

The lifecycle begins with user registration and onboarding, where customers create an account to access a service or platform. A frictionless onboarding process is essential for user engagement, as complex registration forms or cumbersome verification steps can deter potential customers. CIAM solutions streamline registration by offering social login, email-based sign-ups, and progressive profiling, allowing businesses to collect essential user data gradually rather than requiring excessive information upfront. Progressive profiling improves the onboarding experience by reducing friction while enabling businesses to gather more details over time as user engagement increases.

Once a customer account is created, authentication becomes a crucial step in the identity lifecycle. Secure authentication mechanisms ensure that only legitimate users can access their accounts while minimizing friction. CIAM platforms support various authentication methods, including traditional username-password combinations, passwordless authentication, biometric verification, and multi-factor authentication (MFA). Adaptive authentication enhances security by assessing risk factors such as device information, location, and user behavior before determining the level of authentication required. If a login attempt appears suspicious, additional security measures such as an MFA challenge can be triggered to protect the user's account.

Authorization follows authentication, determining what a customer can access within a digital platform. Role-based access control (RBAC) and attribute-based access control (ABAC) help businesses enforce fine-grained access policies based on user attributes, roles, and contextual factors. CIAM solutions enable dynamic authorization adjustments, ensuring that access permissions are continuously evaluated based on changes in user behavior, subscription levels, or security policies. This ensures that customers can access only the resources they are entitled to while preventing unauthorized access to sensitive information.

Profile management is an ongoing process in the customer identity lifecycle. Users must be able to update their personal information, change passwords, configure authentication preferences, and manage privacy settings through self-service portals. Providing intuitive self-service options reduces the need for customer support interactions while empowering users to maintain their own accounts. CIAM solutions enable secure profile management by enforcing data validation, monitoring account changes, and ensuring compliance with data protection regulations such as the General Data Protection Regulation (GDPR) and the California Consumer Privacy Act (CCPA).

Consent management plays a significant role in customer identity lifecycle management, especially in an era where data privacy is a top concern. Customers expect transparency regarding how their personal data is collected, stored, and used. CIAM platforms facilitate consent management by allowing users to grant, modify, or withdraw their consent for data processing activities. Businesses must ensure that consent preferences are stored securely and can be retrieved upon request to demonstrate compliance with privacy regulations. Providing users with control over their data builds trust and enhances customer relationships.

Throughout the lifecycle, continuous monitoring and identity governance ensure security and compliance. Businesses must track user activity, detect anomalies, and prevent unauthorized access attempts. CIAM solutions leverage artificial intelligence and machine learning to analyze login patterns, detect suspicious behavior, and flag potential security threats. Real-time monitoring enables organizations to respond to security incidents promptly, protecting customer identities from fraud and identity theft. Additionally, businesses can generate audit logs and compliance reports to meet regulatory requirements and maintain transparency.

Account recovery and remediation are critical components of identity lifecycle management. Customers often forget passwords, lose access to authentication devices, or encounter security issues that require account recovery. CIAM solutions offer secure recovery options, including password reset mechanisms, backup authentication methods, and account verification through trusted contacts. Businesses must implement secure and user-friendly recovery processes to prevent account takeovers while ensuring that legitimate users can regain access to their accounts with minimal disruption.

As customer identities evolve, businesses must periodically review and update identity attributes, access permissions, and authentication policies. Lifecycle management ensures that outdated or unnecessary access privileges are revoked, reducing security risks associated with inactive accounts. Automated identity governance processes help organizations enforce policies such as session timeouts, periodic password changes, and access reviews. By maintaining up-to-date identity records, businesses enhance security while improving the accuracy of user data.

Deprovisioning is the final stage in customer identity lifecycle management, ensuring that inactive or terminated accounts are securely handled. Customers may choose to close their accounts voluntarily, or businesses may need to deactivate accounts due to inactivity, policy violations, or security concerns. CIAM platforms facilitate secure deprovisioning by permanently deleting user data or anonymizing records in compliance with data protection regulations. Providing users with the ability to delete their accounts enhances trust and demonstrates a commitment to privacy.

Businesses implementing comprehensive identity lifecycle management strategies benefit from improved security, regulatory compliance, and enhanced user experience. A well-managed identity lifecycle reduces identity fraud, prevents unauthorized access, and ensures that customer data remains accurate and secure. By leveraging CIAM solutions to automate identity lifecycle processes, businesses create a seamless and secure digital experience while maintaining compliance with evolving security and privacy requirements.

User Registration and Onboarding

User registration and onboarding are critical components of Customer Identity and Access Management (CIAM) that shape the first interaction between a customer and a digital service. A well-designed registration and onboarding process ensures a smooth user experience while maintaining security and compliance. Businesses must strike a balance between simplicity and security to maximize user adoption while minimizing friction.

The registration process is the first step in the customer journey, where users create an account to access a service or platform. A cumbersome registration experience can lead to user abandonment, while an intuitive and seamless process encourages engagement. CIAM solutions optimize registration by offering multiple sign-up options, including email-based registration, social login, and federated identity authentication. Allowing users to register with an existing identity provider, such as Google, Facebook, or Apple, simplifies the process by reducing the need to create new credentials. Social login also enhances security by leveraging trusted authentication mechanisms while streamlining account creation.

Progressive profiling is a key strategy in modern user registration workflows. Instead of requiring customers to fill out long forms upfront, businesses can collect essential information during initial registration and request additional details over time. This approach reduces friction, improves conversion rates, and ensures that users do not feel overwhelmed by excessive data entry requirements. As customers engage more with the platform, they can gradually provide more information, enabling businesses to personalize their experience while maintaining compliance with data protection regulations.

Security and compliance are essential considerations during registration. Businesses must verify user identities while ensuring that registration processes do not expose vulnerabilities. Email verification, SMS-based one-time passwords (OTPs), and CAPTCHA challenges help prevent fake account creation, bot attacks, and fraudulent registrations. Implementing risk-based authentication allows businesses to assess the legitimacy of a registration attempt based on factors such as location, device fingerprinting, and behavioral analysis. If suspicious activity is detected, additional verification steps can be triggered to ensure the authenticity of the user.

Consent management is an integral part of the registration process, particularly in regions governed by data protection regulations such as the General Data Protection Regulation (GDPR) and the California Consumer Privacy Act (CCPA). Customers must be informed about how their data will be used and given the option to grant or deny specific permissions. CIAM solutions provide built-in consent management tools that allow users to review, modify, and withdraw their consent preferences. Transparent data policies build trust and ensure that businesses remain compliant with regulatory requirements.

User onboarding extends beyond registration by guiding customers through their initial interactions with the platform. A well-structured onboarding experience helps users understand key features, configure their account settings, and complete any necessary identity verification steps. Businesses that invest in a structured onboarding process improve user retention and engagement by ensuring that customers can quickly realize the value of the service.

Personalized onboarding flows enhance user experience by tailoring the process based on individual preferences and behavior. New users may receive interactive tutorials, product recommendations, or guided walkthroughs to help them navigate the platform effectively. Adaptive onboarding adjusts the experience based on user actions, ensuring that customers receive relevant information without unnecessary steps.

Account verification is a critical aspect of onboarding that ensures user authenticity while preventing fraudulent activity. Businesses often require identity verification through email confirmation, phone number verification, or document authentication, depending on the level of security required. Financial institutions, healthcare providers, and e-commerce platforms may implement additional Know Your Customer (KYC) procedures to verify user identities before granting access to sensitive services.

Multi-factor authentication (MFA) can be introduced during onboarding to enhance security. While requiring MFA at the initial registration stage may create friction, businesses can encourage users to enable additional security features as part of the onboarding process. Providing incentives, such as enhanced account protection or exclusive features, can motivate users to adopt stronger authentication methods. Offering multiple authentication options, such as biometric authentication, authenticator apps, or hardware security keys, allows users to choose the method that best suits their needs.

Seamless integration across devices and platforms is essential for a consistent onboarding experience. Users should be able to start the registration process on one device and continue on another without losing progress. CIAM solutions enable cross-device session continuity, allowing customers to switch between web applications, mobile apps, and connected devices effortlessly. This capability is particularly important for businesses offering omnichannel experiences, where users engage with services through multiple touchpoints.

Personalization plays a key role in user onboarding by ensuring that customers receive relevant content and recommendations based on their preferences and behavior. CIAM solutions integrate with customer data platforms and analytics tools to deliver personalized onboarding experiences. Businesses can segment users based on demographic information, engagement history, and usage patterns to provide customized onboarding flows that enhance user satisfaction and retention.

Providing users with self-service account management capabilities empowers them to take control of their identity and security settings. Customers should have the ability to update personal information, configure authentication preferences, manage linked accounts, and review consent settings through an intuitive user interface. Self-service options reduce reliance on customer support teams while improving overall user satisfaction.

Monitoring and optimizing the registration and onboarding process is essential for continuous improvement. Businesses must analyze user behavior, track abandonment rates, and identify pain points in the onboarding journey. A/B testing different registration flows, experimenting with UI/UX changes, and gathering user feedback help refine the process and improve conversion rates. CIAM solutions provide analytics and reporting tools that offer insights into user engagement, authentication trends, and security risks, enabling businesses to make data-driven decisions.

A successful user registration and onboarding strategy creates a positive first impression, enhances security, and fosters long-term customer relationships. Businesses that prioritize a seamless, secure, and personalized onboarding experience build trust, improve retention, and drive engagement. By leveraging CIAM capabilities, organizations can optimize the customer journey, ensuring that users can register, authenticate, and onboard with minimal friction while maintaining high-security standards.

Self-Service Account Management

Self-service account management is a fundamental component of Customer Identity and Access Management (CIAM) that empowers users to take control of their accounts without relying on customer support. Providing customers with intuitive, secure, and efficient self-service options enhances user experience, reduces operational costs, and strengthens overall security. Businesses that implement self-service account management enable users to manage their identities, update personal information, configure authentication preferences, and control privacy settings with ease.

Modern digital users expect convenience and autonomy when managing their online accounts. Traditional account management processes that require customer support intervention for simple tasks, such as password resets or profile updates, create friction and lead to frustration. Self-service portals eliminate these inefficiencies by allowing customers to perform essential account management functions independently. A well-designed self-service experience reduces the need for direct customer service interactions while ensuring that users can quickly and securely access their accounts whenever needed.

One of the most common self-service features in CIAM is password management. Users frequently forget passwords, and without an efficient recovery process, account access issues can lead to abandonment or dissatisfaction. Self-service password reset mechanisms enable users to regain access without contacting support. Businesses implement secure password recovery methods, including email-based reset links, SMS one-time passcodes (OTPs), and authenticator app verification. To enhance security, CIAM platforms integrate risk-based authentication to detect unusual password reset requests and apply additional verification steps when necessary.

Multi-factor authentication (MFA) configuration is another critical aspect of self-service account management. Users should be able to enable, disable, or modify their MFA preferences based on their security needs. A flexible self-service interface allows customers to select authentication methods such as biometric verification, push notifications, hardware security keys, or time-based OTPs. By giving users control over their security settings, businesses encourage the adoption of stronger authentication mechanisms while reducing the risk of account compromise.

Profile management is an essential self-service feature that allows users to update their personal information, including names, email addresses, phone numbers, and mailing addresses. Businesses must ensure that these updates are handled securely, verifying user identity before allowing changes to critical account details. Self-service profile management also extends to managing linked accounts, where users can connect or disconnect third-party authentication providers, such as social login credentials or federated identity accounts. Providing visibility into linked accounts ensures transparency and enhances user trust.

Consent and privacy management play a significant role in self-service account management, particularly in compliance with data protection regulations such as the General Data Protection Regulation (GDPR) and the California Consumer Privacy Act (CCPA). Users must have the ability to review, modify, or withdraw consent for data collection and processing activities. Self-service portals should include clear options for managing marketing preferences, cookie settings, and third-party data sharing agreements. Businesses that provide transparent privacy controls empower users to make informed decisions about their data, fostering trust and regulatory compliance.

Account activity monitoring is another crucial self-service capability that enhances security and user confidence. Customers should be able to view their login history, device activity, and recent authentication attempts to detect any unauthorized access. CIAM solutions integrate real-time session management, allowing users to terminate suspicious sessions or revoke access to unrecognized devices. Providing self-service security insights strengthens user awareness and encourages proactive account protection.

Linked device and session management further enhance self-service capabilities by allowing users to control their active sessions across multiple platforms. Customers who log in from multiple devices, such as smartphones, tablets, and desktops, should have visibility into their connected sessions. If a user notices an unauthorized session, they should be able to revoke access instantly through their self-service dashboard. This feature prevents account takeovers and improves security without requiring direct support intervention.

User account recovery is a critical aspect of self-service account management, ensuring that customers can regain access in case of account lockouts, lost authentication devices, or forgotten credentials. Businesses implement secure account recovery workflows that allow users to verify their identity through secondary email addresses, phone verification, security questions, or backup authentication methods. Offering multiple recovery options improves accessibility while maintaining security standards.

Subscription and service preferences also fall under self-service account management. Customers should be able to manage their subscription plans, payment methods, and service preferences without needing to contact customer support. Providing self-service billing management options, such as updating payment details, canceling subscriptions, or adjusting service levels, enhances customer satisfaction and reduces operational overhead for businesses.

Accessibility and user-friendly design are essential in self-service account management. CIAM solutions must ensure that self-service portals are intuitive, mobile-friendly, and accessible to users with disabilities. Implementing responsive design principles, clear navigation, and multi-language support improves usability for a diverse customer base. Businesses that prioritize accessibility in self-service account management create a more inclusive digital experience.

Security remains a top priority in self-service account management. While empowering users with control over their accounts, businesses must implement safeguards to prevent unauthorized changes and fraud. Secure authentication methods, risk-based access controls, and anomaly detection mechanisms ensure that self-service actions are protected against abuse. Implementing session timeouts, IP restrictions, and account lockout policies adds an extra layer of security while maintaining usability.

Analytics and monitoring help businesses optimize self-service account management. CIAM platforms provide insights into user interactions, common account management issues, and friction points within the self-service experience. Businesses can use this data to refine user flows, improve authentication efficiency, and enhance overall customer satisfaction. Continuous improvement based on user behavior and feedback ensures that self-service features remain effective and user-friendly.

A well-implemented self-service account management strategy reduces customer support costs, enhances security, and improves user satisfaction. Businesses that prioritize self-service capabilities empower users to manage their accounts efficiently while maintaining control over their security and privacy settings. CIAM solutions that offer intuitive, secure, and accessible self-service portals create a frictionless customer experience, fostering trust, engagement, and long-term loyalty.

Progressive Profiling for Better CX

Progressive profiling is an essential strategy in Customer Identity and Access Management (CIAM) that enables businesses to collect user information gradually instead of requiring extensive data entry at the time of registration. This approach enhances customer experience (CX) by reducing friction during onboarding while allowing businesses to gather relevant insights over time. By leveraging progressive profiling, organizations create personalized, engaging, and data-driven interactions without overwhelming users with long forms or intrusive requests.

Traditional registration processes often require users to provide a significant amount of personal information before gaining access to a service. Lengthy sign-up forms can deter potential customers, leading to high abandonment rates and lost engagement opportunities. Progressive profiling solves this challenge by requesting only essential details during initial registration and gradually collecting additional data as users interact with the platform. This step-by-step approach enhances user convenience, making it more likely that customers will complete the onboarding process and remain engaged with the service.

Businesses that implement progressive profiling benefit from improved data quality and customer insights. When users are asked to provide too much information upfront, they may enter incorrect or incomplete data to expedite the registration process. By collecting data progressively, businesses ensure that users provide accurate and relevant information based on their actual engagement with the service. This method leads to better personalization, targeted marketing, and improved customer segmentation.

One of the key advantages of progressive profiling is its ability to enhance personalization without disrupting the user experience. As users engage with a platform, businesses can present contextual prompts to collect additional details such as preferences, interests, and behavioral patterns. For example, an e-commerce platform may initially ask for a user's name and email but later request product preferences, favorite brands, or shopping habits. By integrating progressive profiling with customer analytics, businesses can deliver tailored recommendations, personalized promotions, and customized content that aligns with individual preferences.

Security and privacy considerations play a critical role in progressive profiling. Customers are increasingly aware of how their data is collected and used, and businesses must be transparent in their data collection practices. CIAM solutions that support progressive profiling include built-in consent management features, allowing users to control their data-sharing preferences. Providing users with the option to update or revoke their consent builds trust and ensures compliance with data protection regulations such as the General Data Protection Regulation (GDPR) and the California Consumer Privacy Act (CCPA).

The implementation of progressive profiling should be seamless and integrated into the user journey. Businesses can use interactive UI elements such as pop-up prompts, in-app surveys, and preference centers to collect additional information at relevant touchpoints. Timing is crucial in progressive profiling; requesting too much information too soon can create frustration, while waiting too long may result in missed opportunities for personalization. The key is to introduce data collection moments naturally, based on user actions and engagement levels.

Progressive profiling is particularly effective in omnichannel customer experiences. Users interact with brands across multiple channels, including websites, mobile apps, social media, and customer support portals. A well-integrated CIAM system ensures that customer profiles remain consistent across all touchpoints, allowing businesses to collect data incrementally without duplicating efforts. For example, a customer who initially registers through a website may later complete their profile through a mobile app or during a live chat session with customer support. Maintaining a unified customer identity across channels enhances the overall experience while improving data accuracy.

Email marketing and customer engagement campaigns benefit significantly from progressive profiling. Instead of sending generic emails, businesses can use collected data to craft personalized messages that resonate with individual users. By understanding customer preferences and behaviors, organizations can deliver relevant content, product recommendations, and loyalty rewards that encourage continued engagement. Progressive profiling enables businesses to move beyond static customer profiles, adapting interactions based on real-time user activity and feedback.

One challenge businesses face when implementing progressive profiling is ensuring that data collection remains user-friendly and non-intrusive. Customers should feel that providing additional information is beneficial rather than obligatory. Gamification techniques, incentives, and exclusive offers can motivate users to complete their profiles voluntarily. For instance, a streaming service might encourage users to select their favorite genres in exchange for personalized content recommendations. A travel booking platform could offer tailored travel suggestions based on preferred destinations provided by the user. These strategies make data collection a value-added experience rather than a requirement.

Automation and artificial intelligence (AI) enhance the effectiveness of progressive profiling. By analyzing user behavior and engagement patterns, AI-powered CIAM solutions can determine the optimal moments to request additional information. Machine learning algorithms help predict user preferences based on past interactions, allowing businesses to refine their data collection strategies dynamically. AI-driven insights also enable organizations to detect changes in user behavior, ensuring that customer profiles remain up to date and relevant.

Regulatory compliance and data governance are critical in progressive profiling, especially when handling sensitive customer information. Businesses must ensure that data collection practices align with industry regulations and security standards. CIAM platforms with robust encryption, access controls, and audit logs help protect customer data while maintaining transparency and accountability. Providing users with clear explanations of how their data will be used fosters trust and reduces concerns about privacy risks.

The long-term benefits of progressive profiling extend beyond improved customer experience and personalization. Businesses gain a competitive advantage by leveraging accurate, real-time customer data to optimize their marketing strategies, product development, and customer support initiatives. A well-executed progressive profiling strategy enhances customer satisfaction, increases engagement, and drives business growth by delivering experiences tailored to individual needs.

Organizations adopting progressive profiling as part of their CIAM strategy create more meaningful interactions with customers while ensuring security, compliance, and data integrity. By collecting information gradually and contextually, businesses can improve personalization efforts, reduce friction in user journeys, and build lasting customer relationships based on trust and engagement.

Consent Management in CIAM

Consent management is a cornerstone of Customer Identity and Access Management (CIAM) that focuses on how businesses collect, store, and manage user permissions for data processing activities. In an era where data privacy is paramount and regulations like the General Data Protection Regulation (GDPR) and the California Consumer Privacy Act (CCPA) enforce strict compliance standards, managing customer consent is not just a regulatory necessity but also a means of building trust and transparency with users. Effective consent management in CIAM ensures that organizations handle personal data responsibly while empowering customers with control over their information.

At the heart of consent management lies the principle of user autonomy. Customers must be given clear choices about how their personal data is used, whether for personalized marketing, sharing with third parties, or enabling specific features. A transparent consent process involves presenting users with concise, understandable information about data collection practices at the moment of data capture. This is often achieved through privacy notices, consent pop-ups, and preference centers where users can easily review and adjust their permissions. CIAM solutions streamline this process, integrating consent management directly into user registration and profile management workflows.

Granular consent is a best practice in CIAM, allowing users to give specific permissions for different types of data processing activities. Rather than a blanket "accept all" approach, granular consent enables users to decide, for example, whether they want their browsing behavior tracked for analytics, their purchase history used for personalized recommendations, or their contact information shared with partners. This level of detail not only aligns with regulatory requirements but also enhances user trust by respecting personal preferences. Businesses benefit from granular consent by gaining more accurate insights into customer behaviors and preferences while maintaining ethical data practices.

Consent lifecycle management is a critical aspect of CIAM, addressing how businesses handle consent over time. User preferences may change, and regulations require that consent be revocable, meaning users must have the ability to withdraw their consent at any time. CIAM platforms enable businesses to maintain dynamic consent records, automatically updating systems when users modify their permissions. This flexibility is essential for ensuring ongoing compliance and respecting user autonomy. For instance, a customer who initially agrees to receive marketing emails should be able to opt-out with ease, with their preferences reflected across all relevant systems in real-time.

A major challenge in consent management is maintaining consistency across multiple channels and touchpoints. Customers interact with brands through websites, mobile apps, customer support, and even physical locations. Ensuring that consent preferences are honored consistently across these diverse environments requires a unified approach to identity management. CIAM solutions centralize consent data, enabling organizations to enforce the same user preferences regardless of where the interaction occurs. This omnichannel consistency strengthens compliance efforts and enhances user experience by preventing conflicting experiences or privacy breaches.

Compliance with global data protection regulations is a driving force behind robust consent management in CIAM. GDPR, CCPA, and other frameworks mandate explicit, informed consent for data processing, especially for sensitive personal information. Businesses must not only capture consent but also document it in a way that can be audited. CIAM platforms support these compliance requirements by generating detailed consent logs that track when and how consent was given, modified, or revoked. These records are invaluable during regulatory audits or in responding to data subject requests, demonstrating that the organization respects user rights and adheres to legal standards.

The user experience (UX) of consent management is crucial. No one enjoys being bombarded with confusing legal jargon or intrusive pop-ups. A well-designed CIAM approach integrates consent requests seamlessly into the user journey, making them as non-disruptive as possible. Consent dialogues should be clear, concise, and actionable, guiding users through their choices with simple language and transparent explanations. Visual cues, such as toggles or checkboxes, help users navigate their options, and default settings should respect privacy by requiring active opt-in rather than pre-checked consent boxes.

For businesses, the benefits of effective consent management go beyond compliance and risk mitigation. It becomes a differentiator in building customer trust and loyalty. In an age where consumers are increasingly aware of and concerned about their digital privacy, brands that prioritize transparent and user-friendly consent practices stand out. Customers are more likely to engage with businesses that respect their preferences and communicate openly about data use. This trust translates into stronger customer relationships, higher retention rates, and a competitive edge in the marketplace.

Automation and integration capabilities of CIAM platforms are vital for scaling consent management. Automated workflows ensure that consent preferences are consistently applied across systems, updated in real time, and monitored for compliance. Integration with marketing platforms, CRM systems, and data warehouses allows consent data to inform personalized experiences while respecting user choices. For example, a user who opts out of behavioral tracking shouldn't receive targeted ads or recommendations based on their browsing activity. CIAM platforms bridge the gap between user preferences and business processes, maintaining alignment with consent policies at all times.

Looking ahead, the landscape of consent management is evolving alongside advances in technology and shifts in regulatory environments. Emerging trends like zero-party data—where users proactively share their preferences and intentions with brands—offer new opportunities for consent-driven personalization. Meanwhile, developments in decentralized identity and blockchain could transform how consent is captured and verified, giving users even greater control over their digital footprints. Businesses that stay ahead of these trends by continuously refining their consent management strategies will be better positioned to navigate the complex terrain of digital privacy and user trust.

CIAM and Data Privacy Regulations

Customer Identity and Access Management (CIAM) plays a crucial role in ensuring compliance with data privacy regulations while enabling businesses to deliver seamless digital experiences. As organizations collect and process vast amounts of personal data, they must adhere to strict legal frameworks designed to protect user privacy and prevent data misuse. Regulations such as the General Data Protection Regulation (GDPR), the California Consumer Privacy Act (CCPA), and other regional laws impose requirements on how businesses handle customer identities, consent, and data security. A well-implemented CIAM strategy helps businesses navigate these regulatory landscapes by enforcing privacy controls, ensuring transparency, and securing sensitive customer information.

One of the primary objectives of data privacy regulations is to give users control over their personal information. Businesses must provide clear and transparent policies regarding data collection, processing, and storage. CIAM solutions enable organizations to implement consent management mechanisms that allow users to grant, modify, or withdraw their consent for data usage. Instead of relying on complex legal agreements, businesses can integrate user-friendly consent forms within registration processes, profile management dashboards, and preference centers. This transparency fosters trust and ensures compliance with regulatory obligations.

GDPR, one of the most comprehensive data protection laws, mandates that businesses collect only the minimum necessary personal data and process it for specific, legitimate purposes. CIAM platforms support these principles by implementing data minimization techniques, ensuring that businesses request only essential user information at each stage of interaction. Progressive profiling strategies further enhance compliance by allowing businesses to collect additional details gradually, based on user engagement and explicit consent. This approach reduces unnecessary data storage, minimizing the risk of regulatory violations and data breaches.

The right to access, rectify, and delete personal data is another critical aspect of data privacy regulations. Under GDPR and similar laws, users have the right to request access to their data, correct inaccuracies, and demand its deletion when it is no longer needed. CIAM platforms facilitate these rights by providing self-service account management features, where users can view, update, and request the deletion of their information without requiring manual intervention from support teams. Automating these processes ensures regulatory compliance while enhancing user experience and reducing administrative burdens.

Data portability is another requirement enforced by privacy regulations, ensuring that users can transfer their data from one service provider to another without unnecessary restrictions. CIAM platforms support data portability by offering structured data export functionalities that allow users to download their personal information in machine-readable formats. This capability aligns with compliance standards while giving customers greater flexibility in managing their digital identities across different platforms and services.

Security is a fundamental component of data privacy regulations, and CIAM solutions enforce robust authentication and access control mechanisms to protect customer data from unauthorized access. Multi-factor authentication (MFA), risk-based authentication, and biometric verification strengthen security while ensuring that only legitimate users can access personal information. CIAM also enables businesses to implement least privilege access policies, ensuring that only authorized personnel can view or process sensitive customer data. These security controls align with regulatory mandates such as the Payment Card Industry Data Security Standard (PCI DSS) and the Health Insurance Portability and Accountability Act (HIPAA), which require businesses to protect customer data through stringent security measures.

Regulatory frameworks also emphasize accountability and auditability, requiring businesses to document their data processing activities and demonstrate compliance during audits or legal inquiries. CIAM solutions provide built-in logging and monitoring capabilities that track user authentication events, consent changes, data access requests, and security incidents. These audit trails help businesses maintain transparency and provide regulators with verifiable records of data protection efforts. Automated compliance reporting tools further streamline regulatory compliance, reducing the complexity of documentation and risk assessment.

CCPA and similar regulations expand on consumer rights by allowing users to opt out of data sales and limit the use of their personal information for targeted advertising. CIAM solutions support these requirements by incorporating preference management features that enable users to configure their data-sharing settings easily. Businesses can implement "Do Not Sell My Personal Information" options within user profiles, ensuring compliance with legal mandates while giving customers greater control over their privacy preferences.

Geographic considerations add another layer of complexity to data privacy compliance. Businesses operating globally must comply with multiple regional data protection laws, each with distinct requirements. CIAM platforms offer geo-fencing capabilities that enforce region-specific privacy policies based on the user's location. For example, users in the European Union may be presented with GDPR-compliant consent forms, while users in California receive CCPA-related disclosures. Dynamic policy enforcement ensures that businesses comply with applicable regulations without disrupting the user experience.

Data residency and cross-border data transfers are significant concerns in privacy compliance. Many regulations, including GDPR, impose restrictions on transferring personal data outside specific jurisdictions unless adequate safeguards are in place. CIAM solutions address this challenge by allowing businesses to store and process customer data in compliant regions, leveraging cloud-based identity management services with localized data centers. Encryption, tokenization, and pseudonymization further enhance data security, ensuring that sensitive information remains protected during cross-border transfers.

Emerging privacy regulations continue to evolve, requiring businesses to stay agile and adapt their CIAM strategies accordingly. The growing adoption of privacy-enhancing technologies, such as decentralized identity and self-sovereign identity (SSI), reflects a shift toward giving users more control over their digital identities. These approaches reduce reliance on centralized identity providers, minimizing data exposure while improving compliance with evolving privacy standards. Businesses that invest in future-proof CIAM solutions position themselves to navigate regulatory changes efficiently while maintaining customer trust.

Strong privacy practices are no longer just a legal requirement; they are a competitive advantage. Consumers are increasingly prioritizing privacy and data security when choosing which businesses to trust. Organizations that proactively implement CIAM solutions with robust privacy controls differentiate themselves in the market, attracting privacy-conscious customers and reducing reputational risks. Prioritizing privacy not only mitigates compliance risks but also strengthens customer relationships and fosters long-term loyalty in an increasingly digital world.

GDPR, CCPA, and Global Compliance

Data privacy regulations have become a fundamental aspect of digital business operations, requiring organizations to handle customer data responsibly while ensuring compliance with evolving legal frameworks. The General Data Protection Regulation (GDPR) and the California Consumer Privacy Act (CCPA) are two of the most influential privacy laws, setting the standard for data protection worldwide. While these regulations have specific geographic scopes, their influence extends globally, as businesses operating across multiple jurisdictions must align their data management practices with various compliance requirements. Organizations that implement a robust Customer Identity and Access Management (CIAM) strategy can effectively navigate these regulations, ensuring data security, transparency, and user control.

The GDPR, enacted by the European Union (EU) in 2018, is one of the most comprehensive data privacy laws in the world. It applies to any organization that collects, processes, or stores personal data of EU residents, regardless of where the business is based. GDPR emphasizes user rights, requiring businesses to obtain explicit consent before collecting personal data, provide transparency in data processing, and ensure users can access, modify, or delete their information upon request. Non-compliance with GDPR can result in severe financial penalties, with fines reaching up to €20 million or 4% of a company's global revenue, whichever is higher.

One of the core principles of GDPR is data minimization, which mandates that businesses collect only the necessary personal data required for specific purposes. CIAM solutions support data minimization by implementing progressive profiling, ensuring that organizations gather information incrementally rather than requiring excessive data collection at the point of registration. This approach reduces risk exposure and enhances user experience while maintaining regulatory compliance.

Another key aspect of GDPR is the right to be forgotten, which allows users to request the deletion of their personal data. Businesses must provide a mechanism for users to exercise this right, ensuring that data is permanently erased from all systems and backups. CIAM platforms facilitate this process by integrating automated workflows that handle data deletion requests while maintaining audit logs to demonstrate compliance. Additionally, businesses must ensure that personal data is stored securely, using encryption and anonymization techniques to protect against unauthorized access.

The CCPA, enacted in California in 2020, shares many similarities with GDPR but introduces unique provisions tailored to consumer rights in the United States. Unlike GDPR, which applies broadly to personal data processing, CCPA focuses specifically on consumer rights regarding data collection, sharing, and sales. Under CCPA, businesses must disclose what personal information they collect, who they share it with, and how consumers can opt out of data sales. The law also grants consumers the right to request access to their data and delete it if they choose.

One of the most significant differences between GDPR and CCPA is the approach to consent. While GDPR requires businesses to obtain explicit user consent before collecting data, CCPA follows an opt-out model, meaning businesses can collect and use personal data unless the user explicitly requests otherwise. This difference impacts how businesses implement consent management in CIAM systems, requiring tailored approaches based on the user's location and applicable regulations. Businesses operating in both the EU and California must ensure that their CIAM platforms support dynamic consent frameworks that adjust based on geographic location and legal requirements.

Another major aspect of CCPA compliance is the "Do Not Sell My Personal Information" requirement, which mandates that businesses provide users with a clear option to opt out of having their data sold to third parties. CIAM platforms enable businesses to implement user preference centers, where consumers can manage their data-sharing preferences seamlessly. Additionally, organizations must maintain records of opt-out requests to demonstrate compliance during audits or legal inquiries.

While GDPR and CCPA set the foundation for data privacy compliance, businesses must also consider other regional and industry-specific regulations. Countries such as Brazil, Canada, and Japan have introduced their own privacy laws, such as the Lei Geral de Proteção de Dados (LGPD), the Personal Information Protection and Electronic Documents Act (PIPEDA), and the Act on the Protection of Personal Information (APPI), respectively. These laws share common principles with GDPR and CCPA but introduce unique compliance requirements tailored to local regulations.

Industry-specific regulations further complicate the compliance landscape. Organizations handling financial data must adhere to the Payment Card Industry Data Security Standard (PCI DSS), while healthcare providers must comply with the Health Insurance Portability and Accountability Act (HIPAA) in the United States. CIAM solutions help businesses unify compliance efforts by enforcing security controls, access policies, and data protection measures that align with multiple regulatory frameworks.

One of the biggest challenges businesses face in global compliance is managing cross-border data transfers. GDPR imposes strict restrictions on transferring personal data outside the EU, requiring organizations to implement safeguards such as Standard Contractual Clauses (SCCs) or rely on adequacy decisions. CIAM platforms address this challenge by supporting data residency requirements, ensuring that customer data is stored in compliant regions based on user location. Businesses must also implement encryption and pseudonymization techniques to protect data in transit and at rest, reducing the risk of regulatory violations.

A well-structured CIAM strategy enables businesses to maintain compliance with global privacy regulations while improving user trust and security. Organizations that adopt automated consent management, user preference centers, and advanced security controls can seamlessly adapt to evolving regulatory requirements. Additionally, businesses must stay informed about emerging privacy laws and updates to existing regulations to ensure ongoing compliance.

By implementing CIAM solutions that align with GDPR, CCPA, and other global privacy laws, businesses protect customer data, mitigate compliance risks, and enhance transparency. Privacy-conscious customers are more likely to engage with brands that prioritize data protection, making compliance not just a legal obligation but also a strategic advantage in an increasingly digital world.

The Role of AI and ML in CIAM

Artificial intelligence (AI) and machine learning (ML) are transforming Customer Identity and Access Management (CIAM) by enhancing security, improving user experience, and automating complex identity-related tasks. As digital interactions continue to grow, businesses must find ways to manage customer identities efficiently while minimizing risks associated with unauthorized access, fraud, and data breaches. AI and ML provide the intelligence needed to analyze user behavior, detect anomalies, and enable adaptive authentication, making CIAM more robust and responsive to evolving cybersecurity threats.

One of the most significant applications of AI and ML in CIAM is in fraud detection and risk-based authentication. Traditional identity management systems rely on static rules to determine access, which can be ineffective against sophisticated attacks. AI-driven risk-based authentication continuously analyzes various factors, such as login location, device type, behavioral patterns, and transaction history, to assess the likelihood of fraudulent activity. If a login attempt deviates from a user's typical behavior—such as logging in from an unusual location or using an unrecognized device—the system can trigger additional security measures like multi-factor authentication (MFA) or biometric verification. This dynamic approach reduces the risk of account takeovers while minimizing unnecessary friction for legitimate users.

Behavioral biometrics powered by ML further enhance CIAM by analyzing unique user interactions, such as typing speed, mouse movements, touchscreen gestures, and even navigation patterns. Unlike traditional authentication methods that rely on static credentials, behavioral biometrics continuously monitor user behavior in real time, detecting subtle deviations that may indicate fraudulent activity. By learning how users typically interact with digital platforms, ML algorithms can flag suspicious activities without disrupting the user experience. This technology is particularly effective in preventing automated bot attacks, credential stuffing, and synthetic identity fraud.

AI-driven identity verification streamlines the onboarding process by automating document authentication and biometric matching. Many businesses require identity verification during account registration, especially in regulated industries like banking, healthcare, and e-commerce. AI-powered CIAM solutions use ML algorithms to analyze government-issued IDs, passports, or driver's licenses, verifying their authenticity against global databases. Facial recognition technology matches the document photo with a live selfie, ensuring that the person creating the account is the rightful owner of the identity. By automating these processes, businesses reduce manual review time, enhance security, and provide a seamless onboarding experience for customers.

Personalization is another key area where AI and ML enhance CIAM. Customers expect a seamless and tailored experience across digital platforms, and identity management plays a crucial role in delivering personalization. AI-powered CIAM solutions analyze user preferences, historical interactions, and behavioral trends to create customized authentication journeys. For example, a returning customer using a familiar device in a trusted location may receive a frictionless login experience, while a high-risk attempt may require additional verification. This adaptive approach balances security and convenience, improving user engagement and retention.

ML also plays a critical role in identity governance by automating access control decisions. Traditional access management relies on predefined roles and permissions, which can become complex and inefficient as businesses scale. AI-driven identity governance analyzes user behavior, role assignments, and access patterns to recommend appropriate access levels. If a user no longer requires certain permissions based on their behavior or job function, the system can suggest revoking access to reduce security risks. By continuously learning from access patterns, AI helps organizations enforce the principle of least privilege, ensuring that users only have access to the resources they need.

AI-driven anomaly detection enhances CIAM security by identifying suspicious activities in real time. Unlike rule-based security systems that rely on predefined thresholds, ML algorithms continuously learn from data to detect deviations from normal behavior. This capability is particularly useful in identifying credential compromise, session hijacking, and unauthorized API access. For example, if a user account suddenly exhibits an unusually high number of login attempts from different IP addresses, the system can automatically block access and notify security teams. This proactive approach helps businesses respond to threats before they escalate into full-scale breaches.

Passwordless authentication is gaining traction in CIAM, and AI plays a crucial role in making it more effective. Traditional passwords are prone to phishing attacks, weak credential usage, and breaches, leading businesses to explore more secure authentication methods. AI-powered authentication systems enable passwordless login by analyzing contextual factors, biometric data, and device intelligence. ML algorithms assess whether a login attempt matches known user behaviors, allowing for secure authentication without requiring passwords. This not only improves security but also enhances user convenience by eliminating password-related frustrations.

AI and ML also improve compliance and regulatory adherence within CIAM. Data privacy laws such as GDPR and CCPA require organizations to implement strong identity management practices, including user consent management and data protection. AI-powered CIAM solutions help businesses automate compliance by tracking consent records, identifying data access anomalies, and ensuring that only authorized individuals handle sensitive information. AI can also generate compliance reports, reducing the burden on security teams and auditors while ensuring that organizations meet regulatory requirements.

Customer support and identity recovery processes benefit significantly from AI-driven automation. Account recovery is a common pain point for users who forget passwords or lose access to authentication devices. AI-powered chatbots and virtual assistants streamline identity recovery by guiding users through secure verification steps, reducing reliance on customer support agents. ML algorithms analyze previous interactions to identify the best recovery methods for individual users, ensuring a frictionless yet secure process. This automation improves user satisfaction while reducing operational costs for businesses.

As AI and ML technologies continue to evolve, their role in CIAM will expand, enabling even more advanced security measures and seamless user experiences. Organizations that integrate AI-driven CIAM solutions gain a competitive edge by enhancing identity security, reducing fraud, and optimizing customer interactions. By leveraging intelligent authentication, adaptive access controls, and continuous learning models, businesses can protect user identities while delivering personalized and frictionless digital experiences.

Risk-Based Authentication and Fraud Prevention

Risk-based authentication (RBA) is a critical component of modern Customer Identity and Access Management (CIAM) that dynamically adjusts security measures based on the risk level of a given authentication attempt. Unlike static authentication methods that apply the same level of security to all users, RBA analyzes contextual factors to determine whether additional verification steps are necessary. By implementing RBA, businesses can enhance security, reduce fraud, and improve user experience by minimizing friction for legitimate users while blocking suspicious activities.

Fraud prevention has become a top priority as cyber threats continue to evolve, with attackers using advanced techniques such as credential stuffing, phishing, and account takeovers to exploit weaknesses in authentication systems. Traditional security approaches, such as passwords and static multi-factor authentication (MFA), are no longer sufficient to prevent unauthorized access. RBA addresses these challenges by continuously assessing login attempts and applying adaptive authentication measures that match the level of risk associated with each request.

The foundation of risk-based authentication is real-time analysis of multiple factors that help determine whether a login attempt is legitimate or potentially fraudulent. These factors include device fingerprinting, IP reputation, geolocation, behavioral biometrics, and historical user activity. If a login attempt originates from a recognized device and location with typical user behavior, the system allows access with minimal friction. However, if an attempt appears unusual—such as a login from an unfamiliar country, a different device, or a sudden change in user behavior—the system triggers additional security measures, such as step-up authentication or transaction verification.

Device fingerprinting plays a crucial role in RBA by analyzing hardware and software characteristics of the device being used for authentication. Each device has unique attributes, including operating system, browser type, screen resolution, and installed plugins. RBA solutions compare these attributes to previously recorded device fingerprints to determine whether the login attempt is coming from a trusted source. If a new or unrecognized device is detected, the system may prompt the user for additional verification to confirm their identity.

IP reputation analysis helps detect fraudulent login attempts by assessing the risk level associated with an IP address. If a login request comes from an IP address that has been flagged for suspicious activities—such as involvement in bot attacks, proxy usage, or previous fraud incidents—the system can deny access or require further authentication. Businesses can also leverage geo-blocking techniques to restrict access from high-risk regions known for cybercrime activities.

Behavioral biometrics enhance fraud prevention by analyzing how users interact with a website or application. RBA solutions track user behaviors such as typing speed, mouse movements, and navigation patterns to establish a behavioral profile. If an authentication attempt deviates significantly from a user's established behavioral norms, the system can flag the request as high risk and take appropriate action. This method is particularly effective in detecting automated bot attacks and fraudulent account takeovers.

Historical user activity provides valuable context for determining authentication risk. RBA systems analyze past login attempts, transaction history, and frequency of account access to identify patterns. If a user typically logs in from the same city using a specific device but suddenly attempts to access their account from a different continent using an unknown device, the system recognizes the anomaly and enforces additional security measures. By continuously learning from past interactions, RBA solutions improve accuracy in detecting fraudulent activities while minimizing false positives.

Step-up authentication is a key mechanism in risk-based authentication, requiring users to complete additional verification steps when high-risk scenarios are detected. This can include multi-factor authentication (MFA), biometric verification, email or SMS-based one-time passcodes (OTPs), or security questions. Step-up authentication ensures that legitimate users can verify their identities while preventing unauthorized access by attackers who may have obtained stolen credentials.

Adaptive authentication enhances user experience by adjusting security requirements dynamically based on risk assessments. For example, a returning user accessing their account from a familiar device in a trusted location may be allowed to log in with minimal authentication steps, while a new device login attempt may require additional verification. This approach reduces friction for trusted users while strengthening security against unauthorized access attempts.

Fraud prevention in CIAM extends beyond authentication to continuous monitoring of user activities post-login. RBA solutions integrate with fraud detection systems to analyze user behavior during transactions, detecting anomalies such as unusual spending patterns, rapid changes in account settings, or multiple failed authentication attempts. If suspicious behavior is detected, the system can initiate real-time interventions, such as account suspension, transaction blocking, or requiring additional identity verification.

Organizations implementing RBA and fraud prevention strategies must also consider regulatory compliance requirements. Data protection laws such as the General Data Protection Regulation (GDPR) and the California Consumer Privacy Act (CCPA) require businesses to implement strong security measures to protect user identities and personal data. By adopting risk-based authentication, businesses demonstrate compliance with regulatory standards while minimizing the risk of data breaches and financial fraud.

AI and machine learning play an increasingly important role in RBA and fraud prevention by continuously analyzing vast amounts of authentication data to identify emerging threats. Machine learning algorithms detect patterns and correlations that human analysts may overlook, allowing RBA systems to evolve and adapt to new attack techniques. AI-driven fraud detection enhances the ability to differentiate between legitimate users and malicious actors, improving security effectiveness without compromising user convenience.

Implementing RBA and fraud prevention in CIAM requires a balance between security and usability. While strong authentication measures protect against cyber threats, excessive security requirements can frustrate users and lead to account abandonment. Businesses must fine-tune risk assessment models to minimize unnecessary authentication challenges while maintaining robust security protections. A user-centric approach ensures that security measures are applied intelligently, reducing friction for genuine customers while blocking fraudulent access attempts.

By leveraging risk-based authentication and advanced fraud prevention techniques, organizations strengthen their CIAM frameworks, protect customer identities, and deliver a seamless yet secure digital experience. Dynamic authentication mechanisms, AI-driven threat detection, and continuous monitoring create a resilient defense against identity fraud while ensuring that users can access services effortlessly. Businesses that integrate RBA effectively enhance trust, reduce fraud-related losses, and maintain compliance with evolving security and privacy regulations.

CIAM and Adaptive Access Controls

Customer Identity and Access Management (CIAM) has evolved beyond static authentication methods to incorporate adaptive access controls that dynamically adjust security measures based on real-time risk assessments. Traditional access management systems apply uniform security policies to all users, often leading to excessive friction for legitimate users or insufficient protection against threats. Adaptive access controls address these challenges by continuously evaluating user behavior, device information, contextual factors, and risk signals to determine the appropriate level of authentication and access.

Adaptive access controls enhance security while maintaining a seamless user experience. Instead of enforcing the same authentication steps for every login attempt, adaptive controls adjust security requirements based on risk levels. For example, a returning customer logging in from a familiar device at a typical location may be granted access with minimal authentication friction, while an attempt from an unrecognized device in a high-risk location may trigger additional verification steps such as multi-factor authentication (MFA) or biometric validation.

Context-aware authentication is a core principle of adaptive access controls. By analyzing contextual attributes such as geographic location, IP address reputation, network type, and device fingerprinting, CIAM platforms can assess the risk associated with each authentication attempt. If an access request originates from a trusted environment, the system can allow a frictionless login. However, if the request is flagged as unusual, adaptive access controls can enforce stronger security measures, such as step-up authentication or session monitoring.

Behavioral analytics play a crucial role in adaptive access controls by analyzing user interactions and detecting deviations from normal patterns. Machine learning models track factors such as keystroke dynamics, navigation habits, mouse movements, and touch gestures to establish a behavioral profile for each user. If an authentication attempt exhibits behavior inconsistent with the user's typical patterns, the system can flag the request as high-risk and require additional verification. This approach helps prevent account takeovers, bot attacks, and credential abuse without disrupting legitimate users.

Device intelligence enhances adaptive access controls by evaluating device-related risk factors. Each device has unique attributes, including operating system version, browser type, installed plugins, and hardware specifications. CIAM platforms use device fingerprinting to recognize known devices and assess the trustworthiness of new ones. If a login attempt is initiated from an unfamiliar or potentially compromised device, the system can prompt additional authentication steps before granting access. This method prevents attackers from using stolen credentials on unauthorized devices while ensuring a smooth experience for users logging in from trusted devices.

Real-time risk scoring is an essential component of adaptive access controls. CIAM platforms assign a risk score to each authentication attempt based on multiple data points, including login frequency, location consistency, transaction history, and previous security incidents. If the risk score exceeds a predefined threshold, the system can enforce additional security measures or temporarily block access until the user confirms their identity. AI-powered risk scoring continuously learns from authentication patterns, improving its accuracy in detecting threats while reducing false positives.

Step-up authentication is a key mechanism within adaptive access controls that increases security dynamically when a higher level of risk is detected. Instead of applying the same authentication requirements to all users, step-up authentication activates only when needed. For example, a user accessing low-risk content may log in with a simple password, but attempting to perform a high-risk action, such as changing account settings or making a financial transaction, may require biometric verification or a one-time passcode. This layered security approach balances usability and protection.

Adaptive access controls also support continuous authentication, ensuring that user sessions remain secure even after initial login. Traditional authentication methods verify user identity only at the point of login, but continuous authentication monitors user behavior throughout a session to detect anomalies. If unusual activity occurs—such as a sudden change in typing speed or navigation patterns—the system can prompt re-authentication, restrict certain actions, or terminate the session altogether. Continuous authentication is especially valuable in preventing session hijacking and insider threats.

Integration with fraud prevention mechanisms strengthens adaptive access controls by enabling proactive threat detection. CIAM platforms analyze login attempts in real time, cross-referencing data with fraud intelligence feeds, blacklisted IP addresses, and suspicious behavioral patterns. If an access attempt matches known fraudulent characteristics, the system can deny access or trigger further identity verification. This approach minimizes the risk of automated attacks, phishing scams, and credential stuffing while maintaining a frictionless experience for trusted users.

Regulatory compliance is another area where adaptive access controls play a crucial role. Data protection regulations such as the General Data Protection Regulation (GDPR) and the California Consumer Privacy Act (CCPA) require businesses to implement strong security measures to protect customer identities. Adaptive access controls help businesses comply with these regulations by ensuring that authentication and access decisions are context-aware, minimizing the risk of unauthorized data exposure while providing users with transparent and secure authentication options.

Organizations implementing adaptive access controls must consider usability and accessibility to ensure inclusivity for all users. While security is a priority, excessive authentication challenges can lead to frustration and account abandonment. CIAM solutions that offer flexible authentication options, such as biometric login, email-based verification, or hardware security keys, allow users to choose their preferred authentication method. Providing self-service security settings empowers users to manage their authentication preferences while maintaining control over their digital identities.

Scalability is another advantage of adaptive access controls in CIAM. Businesses with large customer bases must handle millions of authentication requests daily without compromising performance. Cloud-based CIAM platforms leverage AI-driven automation and scalable infrastructure to process authentication decisions in real time, ensuring that security controls adapt to demand fluctuations and peak usage periods. This scalability is particularly important for e-commerce, financial services, and subscription-based platforms that experience seasonal or event-driven traffic spikes.

Adaptive access controls provide a strategic advantage for businesses seeking to enhance security while delivering seamless user experiences. By leveraging real-time risk assessment, behavioral analytics, device intelligence, and continuous authentication, organizations can protect customer identities against evolving threats without introducing unnecessary friction. CIAM platforms that integrate adaptive access controls enable businesses to build trust with customers, reduce fraud risks, and maintain compliance with global security and privacy regulations.

Customer Identity Governance and Administration

Customer Identity Governance and Administration (IGA) is an essential component of Customer Identity and Access Management (CIAM), ensuring that businesses manage customer identities securely while maintaining compliance with regulatory standards. Effective identity governance provides visibility, control, and security over customer data, access permissions, and identity lifecycles. As businesses scale their digital services, the ability to manage millions of customer identities efficiently while preventing unauthorized access becomes a strategic necessity.

Governance in CIAM revolves around defining policies and enforcing controls that dictate how customer identities are created, stored, accessed, and deactivated. Unlike workforce identity governance, which focuses on employee access within an organization, customer identity governance must address large-scale, dynamic user populations with diverse authentication and authorization requirements. Businesses must implement identity governance frameworks that protect customer data while enabling seamless and secure access to digital services.

A fundamental aspect of customer identity governance is lifecycle management, which oversees the entire identity journey from registration to deactivation. Identity lifecycle management ensures that customer data remains accurate, secure, and compliant with regulatory requirements. When a customer creates an account, CIAM systems enforce verification protocols to authenticate their identity. Throughout the customer's engagement with the platform, access permissions must be continuously reviewed and updated based on changes in user behavior, security risks, or evolving business policies. When a customer no longer requires access, their identity should be properly deactivated or anonymized to prevent security vulnerabilities.

Access control plays a critical role in customer identity governance. CIAM solutions enforce access policies that define what users can do within a platform based on predefined rules and risk assessments. Role-based access control (RBAC) assigns permissions based on user roles, ensuring that different types of users—such as basic consumers, premium members, or business partners—receive appropriate access levels. Attribute based access control (ABAC) takes a more dynamic approach by evaluating contextual factors such as location, device type, and transaction history before granting access. These mechanisms prevent unauthorized access while ensuring that customers can navigate services without unnecessary restrictions.

Consent management is another crucial element of identity governance, particularly in an era of stringent data privacy regulations. Customers must have control over how their personal data is used, and businesses must document user consent in a way that is accessible and auditable. CIAM platforms provide self-service consent management portals where users can modify their data-sharing preferences, opt out of marketing communications, or request data deletion. Automated consent tracking ensures that businesses remain compliant with regulations such as the General Data Protection Regulation (GDPR) and the California Consumer Privacy Act (CCPA), reducing the risk of legal penalties and reputational damage.

Data protection is at the core of identity governance, requiring businesses to implement strong security measures to prevent unauthorized access, breaches, and data leaks. CIAM platforms enforce encryption, tokenization, and anonymization techniques to safeguard customer information. Encryption protects data both at rest and in transit, ensuring that even if unauthorized parties gain access to a database, the information remains unreadable. Tokenization replaces sensitive data with unique identifiers, minimizing exposure in cases where customer data is processed or shared with third-party services.

Identity governance also involves continuous monitoring and auditing to detect anomalies and enforce security policies. CIAM solutions integrate with security information and event management (SIEM) systems to analyze login trends, authentication attempts, and access patterns. Anomalous activities—such as repeated failed login attempts, access requests from high-risk locations, or sudden changes in user behavior—trigger security alerts and automated responses. Businesses can enforce real-time security actions, such as step-up authentication, session termination, or account suspension, to prevent fraudulent access.

Regulatory compliance is a major driver of identity governance, as businesses must adhere to industry-specific and regional data protection laws. In addition to GDPR and CCPA, organizations operating in financial services must comply with the Payment Card Industry Data Security Standard (PCI DSS), while healthcare providers must meet the Health Insurance Portability and Accountability Act (HIPAA) requirements. CIAM platforms streamline compliance by maintaining audit logs, enforcing secure authentication methods, and enabling organizations to demonstrate adherence to regulatory mandates.

User self-service capabilities enhance governance by allowing customers to manage their own identity and access settings. Instead of relying on customer support teams to handle account updates, password resets, or security configurations, businesses can provide intuitive self-service portals where users can make changes independently. Self-service options improve efficiency while reducing administrative overhead, ensuring that customers can access and control their personal data securely.

Automation plays a significant role in modern identity governance, reducing manual effort while increasing accuracy and efficiency. CIAM solutions leverage artificial intelligence (AI) and machine learning (ML) to detect potential identity-related risks, optimize access control decisions, and enforce governance policies dynamically. Automated identity governance eliminates inconsistencies, reduces human error, and ensures that policies are consistently applied across all customer interactions.

Scalability is a key consideration in customer identity governance, as businesses must manage growing volumes of user identities without compromising security or performance. Cloud-based CIAM platforms provide elastic scalability, allowing organizations to handle millions of authentication requests and identity verifications in real time. Whether a business is expanding into new markets, launching new services, or integrating with third-party applications, identity governance ensures that security and compliance are maintained at scale.

Cross-channel identity management is essential for businesses operating across multiple digital platforms, including websites, mobile apps, and IoT devices. CIAM solutions centralize identity governance, ensuring that customer identities remain consistent and secure across all touchpoints. Unified identity policies prevent fragmentation, allowing users to authenticate seamlessly while maintaining a single, secure identity across different platforms.

Customer identity governance is not just about security and compliance—it also impacts user trust and brand reputation. Businesses that prioritize strong identity governance practices demonstrate their commitment to protecting customer data and providing secure digital experiences. Transparency in identity management, clear privacy policies, and robust access controls enhance user confidence, fostering long-term customer relationships.

By integrating identity governance with CIAM, businesses establish a structured approach to managing customer identities while ensuring security, compliance, and scalability. Governance frameworks provide the necessary controls to mitigate risks, prevent unauthorized access, and maintain regulatory alignment. A well-implemented identity governance strategy enables businesses to protect customer data, enhance security, and deliver seamless digital experiences that align with both user expectations and legal requirements.

Secure APIs and CIAM Integration

Secure APIs play a fundamental role in Customer Identity and Access Management (CIAM) by enabling seamless authentication, authorization, and data exchange across digital services. As businesses adopt omnichannel strategies and cloud-based architectures, integrating CIAM with APIs ensures secure access to applications, platforms, and third-party services. A well-implemented CIAM API strategy enhances security, scalability, and user experience while protecting sensitive customer data from unauthorized access and cyber threats.

APIs act as the connective tissue between identity providers, applications, and external services, allowing businesses to centralize authentication and identity management. CIAM solutions rely on APIs to facilitate user registration, authentication, profile management, consent handling, and access control. By integrating CIAM with APIs, businesses can create a unified digital identity ecosystem where customers authenticate once and gain access to multiple services without repeated logins. This approach reduces friction while maintaining strong security measures.

Security is a top priority when exposing CIAM functionalities through APIs. Unauthorized access to identity-related APIs can lead to account takeovers, data breaches, and compliance violations. Implementing robust API security mechanisms ensures that authentication and authorization requests are processed securely. OAuth 2.0, OpenID Connect (OIDC), and Security Assertion Markup Language (SAML) are industry-standard protocols that enable secure identity federation, token-based authentication, and cross-platform identity verification. These protocols ensure that authentication requests are properly validated, preventing unauthorized access to user data.

OAuth 2.0 is widely used in CIAM API integration to enable secure delegated access. Instead of requiring users to share passwords across multiple applications, OAuth 2.0 issues access tokens that grant permission to specific resources. When a customer logs in using a third-party identity provider, OAuth 2.0 ensures that only the necessary access permissions are granted. This minimizes security risks while enhancing user convenience by enabling Single Sign-On (SSO) across multiple services.

OIDC extends OAuth 2.0 by adding an authentication layer that allows businesses to verify user identities. Through ID tokens, OIDC provides standardized user identity attributes, enabling seamless integration between CIAM platforms and external applications. This approach ensures that businesses can retrieve verified identity information without exposing sensitive credentials. OIDC simplifies authentication workflows, reducing implementation complexity while enhancing security and interoperability.

API security best practices such as token-based authentication, rate limiting, and encryption play a crucial role in protecting CIAM integrations. JSON Web Tokens (JWT) are commonly used in CIAM API authentication to securely transmit identity information between services. JWTs are digitally signed, ensuring that authentication tokens cannot be tampered with or forged. By implementing short-lived tokens with automatic expiration, businesses mitigate the risk of token theft and replay attacks.

Rate limiting and API throttling help prevent abuse and distributed denial-of-service (DDoS) attacks. CIAM APIs that handle authentication and identity verification requests must be protected against excessive traffic from malicious actors. Rate limiting restricts the number of API calls per user or IP address within a specified timeframe, reducing the risk of brute-force attacks and credential stuffing. API gateways enforce rate limiting policies, ensuring that identity-related requests do not overwhelm CIAM infrastructure.

Encryption ensures that sensitive identity data remains protected during API transactions. Transport Layer Security (TLS) encrypts API communications, preventing data interception and man-in-the-middle attacks. Strong encryption algorithms such as AES-256 protect customer identity attributes, ensuring that data remains secure even if intercepted. Businesses must enforce end-to-end encryption across all CIAM API interactions to maintain data confidentiality and integrity.

Zero Trust principles enhance API security by enforcing continuous verification at every request. Unlike traditional perimeter-based security models, Zero Trust assumes that all API requests must be authenticated, authorized, and validated before access is granted. CIAM API security integrates with identity verification mechanisms, ensuring that authentication tokens are validated against risk-based policies. Adaptive authentication further strengthens security by requiring additional verification for high-risk API requests.

Secure API integration also enables CIAM to support multi-factor authentication (MFA) across applications. Instead of implementing authentication separately for each service, businesses can leverage CIAM APIs to enforce MFA policies consistently. API-based MFA enables seamless authentication workflows, allowing users to verify their identities using SMS codes, authenticator apps, biometrics, or push notifications. This approach enhances security without introducing unnecessary friction.

CIAM APIs facilitate seamless integration with third-party applications, partner ecosystems, and IoT devices. Businesses that operate multiple services require centralized identity management to ensure that user authentication remains consistent across platforms. API-based CIAM integration enables organizations to provide unified identity experiences, where customers can log in once and access multiple digital services without additional authentication.

Compliance with data privacy regulations is a critical aspect of CIAM API security. Regulations such as the General Data Protection Regulation (GDPR) and the California Consumer Privacy Act (CCPA) require businesses to protect user identities and control access to personal data. CIAM APIs must implement consent management mechanisms that allow users to control how their data is shared. API-based consent tracking ensures that user preferences are consistently enforced across all integrated applications, reducing compliance risks.

Automated monitoring and logging enhance API security by detecting anomalies and potential threats. CIAM platforms integrate with Security Information and Event Management (SIEM) systems to analyze API request patterns, identify suspicious activity, and enforce real-time security policies. If an API request exhibits unusual behavior—such as repeated failed authentication attempts or access from a high-risk IP address—the system can trigger alerts, enforce additional authentication, or block the request altogether.

Scalability is another key benefit of CIAM API integration. Businesses with large user bases require scalable authentication solutions that handle high volumes of login requests without performance degradation. API-driven CIAM architectures support cloud scalability, enabling businesses to handle peak traffic loads efficiently. Load balancing and auto-scaling mechanisms ensure that authentication services remain responsive, even during high-demand periods such as product launches or seasonal events.

By implementing secure APIs for CIAM integration, businesses enhance security, streamline authentication workflows, and enable seamless digital experiences. API-driven identity management ensures that user authentication, access control, and consent preferences remain consistent across applications, reducing security risks while improving customer trust. As businesses continue to expand their digital ecosystems, secure CIAM API integration remains essential for protecting identities and enabling frictionless user access.

Customer Identity and Omnichannel Strategies

Customer Identity and Access Management (CIAM) plays a crucial role in enabling seamless omnichannel experiences by ensuring that users can securely access services across multiple platforms without friction. Businesses operating in a digital-first landscape must provide a unified identity experience that allows customers to interact consistently across websites, mobile apps, call centers, IoT devices, and in-person transactions. By integrating CIAM with omnichannel strategies, organizations enhance customer engagement, improve personalization, and strengthen security while maintaining regulatory compliance.

A fundamental challenge in omnichannel identity management is ensuring that users can transition between different platforms without needing to reauthenticate or re-enter their credentials multiple times. Single Sign-On (SSO) enables customers to log in once and access multiple services without disruption. Whether they begin a shopping session on a mobile app, continue on a desktop website, and finalize their purchase through a voice assistant, SSO ensures a seamless authentication experience. CIAM solutions provide centralized identity management that supports SSO across all digital touchpoints, reducing user frustration while enhancing security.

Identity federation further simplifies omnichannel authentication by allowing businesses to integrate third-party identity providers. Customers prefer to use existing credentials from providers such as Google, Apple, or Facebook instead of creating new accounts for each service. By supporting identity federation, businesses reduce friction in the registration process while ensuring that authentication remains secure and user-friendly. This approach improves conversion rates by minimizing abandoned registrations caused by complex onboarding requirements.

Consistency in identity management is essential for delivering personalized omnichannel experiences. CIAM solutions enable businesses to maintain a unified customer profile that aggregates user preferences, transaction history, and behavioral data across all touchpoints. A customer who browses products on a mobile app should receive personalized recommendations when they switch to a desktop or interact with a customer support representative. Unified identity management ensures that businesses can offer contextual experiences based on real-time customer interactions.

Security remains a top priority in omnichannel strategies, as customers expect frictionless yet secure authentication across devices. Adaptive authentication dynamically adjusts security requirements based on contextual factors such as device type, geolocation, and risk level. A trusted login from a familiar device may require minimal authentication steps, while an attempt from an unfamiliar location might trigger multi-factor authentication (MFA). CIAM platforms integrate risk-based authentication to ensure that security measures align with user behavior without introducing unnecessary friction.

Omnichannel CIAM also enables businesses to implement cross-channel consent management, ensuring that user privacy preferences remain consistent regardless of where they interact. Data protection regulations such as the General Data Protection Regulation (GDPR) and the California Consumer Privacy Act (CCPA) require organizations to provide customers with control over their data. CIAM solutions centralize consent management, allowing users to set their preferences once and have them enforced across all platforms. If a customer opts out of marketing emails via a mobile app, the preference should automatically apply to website interactions and call center communications.

Customer support interactions benefit from omnichannel identity management by enabling secure authentication across different service channels. A user reaching out to a call center should not need to repeat authentication steps if they have already verified their identity through a mobile app. CIAM solutions integrate with customer support systems to provide agents with secure, real-time access to user profiles while ensuring that authentication remains consistent across chatbots, email, and live support channels.

IoT and smart devices introduce additional complexity to omnichannel identity management. Customers interact with businesses through connected devices such as smart TVs, wearables, and home automation systems, requiring secure identity authentication across these environments. CIAM solutions support device identity management, ensuring that user credentials can be securely linked to IoT ecosystems. Whether a customer logs in through a mobile app or a voice assistant, their identity remains verified across all digital interactions.

Omnichannel loyalty programs benefit from unified customer identity management by ensuring that rewards and personalized offers are accessible across all platforms. A customer earning loyalty points through in-store purchases should see their updated balance reflected in a mobile app and receive relevant promotions when shopping online. CIAM platforms facilitate seamless loyalty program integration, allowing businesses to create personalized engagement strategies based on real-time customer identity data.

Retail and e-commerce businesses rely heavily on omnichannel identity management to drive personalized shopping experiences. Customers expect continuity when switching between online and offline interactions, such as adding items to a cart on a mobile app and completing the purchase in-store using a digital wallet. CIAM solutions enable unified authentication across digital and physical environments, ensuring that customers receive a seamless shopping journey regardless of the channel they choose.

Financial services and banking institutions leverage CIAM for omnichannel security and compliance. Customers accessing banking services through web portals, mobile apps, ATMs, and in-branch visits require a consistent identity verification process. CIAM platforms integrate biometric authentication, passwordless login, and risk-based security measures to ensure that financial transactions remain secure across all digital and physical touchpoints. Strong identity verification enhances customer trust while protecting against fraud and account takeovers.

Entertainment and streaming services benefit from omnichannel identity management by ensuring that users can access content across multiple devices without authentication barriers. A customer watching a show on a smart TV should be able to resume playback seamlessly on a smartphone or tablet without logging in again. CIAM platforms synchronize user sessions, preferences, and authentication states across all devices, delivering a frictionless entertainment experience.

Omnichannel identity strategies also play a key role in healthcare services, where patients require secure access to medical records, telehealth consultations, and in-person appointments. CIAM solutions provide secure identity verification across patient portals, mobile health apps, and electronic health record (EHR) systems. Patients can manage their healthcare data, schedule appointments, and communicate with providers while ensuring that their identity remains protected through strong authentication controls.

Scalability is a critical factor in omnichannel CIAM, as businesses must handle millions of authentication requests across multiple platforms without performance degradation. Cloud-based CIAM solutions offer elastic scalability, ensuring that authentication services remain responsive during peak traffic periods. Whether a business experiences seasonal surges or rapid growth, CIAM platforms dynamically scale to accommodate high volumes of user interactions while maintaining security and performance.

By integrating CIAM with omnichannel strategies, businesses create seamless, secure, and personalized digital experiences that enhance customer engagement and trust. A well-executed omnichannel identity management approach ensures that users can navigate multiple platforms effortlessly while maintaining security, privacy, and convenience across all digital touchpoints.

CIAM for Mobile and IoT Devices

Customer Identity and Access Management (CIAM) plays a crucial role in securing and managing user identities across mobile and Internet of Things (IoT) devices. As digital interactions expand beyond traditional web applications, businesses must ensure seamless authentication, authorization, and data protection across smartphones, tablets, smart home devices, wearables, and industrial IoT systems. Implementing a robust CIAM strategy for mobile and IoT environments enhances user experience, prevents unauthorized access, and safeguards personal data while maintaining compliance with security and privacy regulations.

Mobile devices have become the primary gateway for customer interactions, making mobile identity management an essential component of CIAM. Unlike desktops, mobile environments introduce additional security challenges such as device fragmentation, varying operating systems, and risks associated with lost or stolen devices. CIAM solutions designed for mobile authentication must support multiple authentication methods, including biometrics, passwordless login, social authentication, and multi-factor authentication (MFA). Mobile biometrics, such as fingerprint scanning and facial recognition, provide a frictionless and secure authentication experience, reducing reliance on traditional passwords while improving security.

Adaptive authentication is particularly important in mobile CIAM implementations. Since users frequently switch between networks, locations, and devices, risk-based authentication mechanisms analyze contextual factors such as geolocation, device reputation, and behavioral patterns to determine authentication requirements dynamically. If a login attempt occurs from a recognized mobile device and location, the CIAM system may grant access with minimal friction. However, if an attempt originates from an unusual location or untrusted network, step-up authentication measures, such as requiring additional verification or MFA, may be enforced to mitigate risks.

Mobile applications also rely on API-based authentication to enable seamless and secure interactions. CIAM platforms integrate with mobile apps using authentication protocols such as OAuth 2.0 and OpenID Connect (OIDC), ensuring secure access without exposing sensitive credentials. OAuth 2.0 enables delegated authentication, allowing mobile applications to authenticate users through third-party identity providers while granting limited access to specific resources. OIDC enhances mobile authentication by providing identity tokens that include verified user information, ensuring secure identity federation across applications and services.

Push notification authentication is an emerging trend in mobile CIAM, replacing traditional SMS-based one-time passwords (OTPs) with secure, app-based authentication requests. When a user attempts to log in, a push notification is sent to their registered mobile device, prompting them to approve or deny the request with a single tap. This method improves security by eliminating risks associated with SIM swapping and phishing attacks while providing a more convenient authentication experience.

IoT devices introduce unique identity management challenges due to their diverse form factors, lack of user interfaces, and limited processing capabilities. Unlike traditional computing devices, many IoT systems operate in headless environments where direct user interaction is minimal or nonexistent. CIAM for IoT must accommodate these constraints by implementing secure device authentication mechanisms that do not rely on traditional username-password authentication models.

Device identity is a critical aspect of IoT security, ensuring that only authorized devices can access networks and services. CIAM solutions assign unique identities to IoT devices using digital certificates, hardware security modules (HSMs), or cryptographic keys. Public Key Infrastructure (PKI) enables IoT devices to authenticate securely using digital certificates, preventing unauthorized access and device impersonation. Certificate-based authentication ensures that devices establish trusted connections without relying on user credentials, reducing security vulnerabilities associated with password-based authentication.

Federated identity management plays a key role in IoT CIAM by enabling seamless integration across multiple IoT ecosystems. Businesses operating large IoT networks must manage identities across various vendors, cloud platforms, and communication protocols. Federated identity allows IoT devices to authenticate using identity providers that support industry standards such as OAuth 2.0, SAML, and OIDC. This approach simplifies identity management by centralizing authentication and access policies while enabling interoperability across different IoT platforms.

Access control in IoT environments must be fine-grained and context-aware, ensuring that devices interact only with authorized resources. Role-based access control (RBAC) and attribute-based access control (ABAC) help enforce security policies by restricting device permissions based on predefined rules, user roles, or contextual conditions. For example, a smart home security camera should grant access only to authorized users while preventing unauthorized remote control. Similarly, industrial IoT sensors monitoring critical infrastructure must restrict access to trusted applications and prevent unauthorized data modifications.

Secure communication is essential for IoT identity management, as many devices transmit sensitive data over public and private networks. CIAM solutions implement encryption protocols such as Transport Layer Security (TLS) to protect data in transit, preventing eavesdropping and man-in-the-middle attacks. End-to-end encryption ensures that identity-related communications between IoT devices, cloud services, and mobile applications remain protected from unauthorized access.

Managing user consent and privacy in mobile and IoT environments requires CIAM solutions to provide clear and accessible privacy controls. Users must have the ability to manage device permissions, opt-in or opt-out of data collection, and review how their personal information is used across mobile apps and IoT platforms. CIAM platforms integrate consent management tools that allow users to configure privacy preferences in real-time, ensuring compliance with regulations such as the General Data Protection Regulation (GDPR) and the California Consumer Privacy Act (CCPA).

Device lifecycle management is a crucial component of CIAM for mobile and IoT ecosystems. Businesses must track and manage device identities from initial registration to decommissioning, ensuring that retired or compromised devices no longer have access to customer accounts or sensitive data. CIAM solutions provide automated deprovisioning workflows that revoke access credentials when a device is lost, stolen, or reaches end-of-life. By enforcing identity lifecycle policies, businesses reduce security risks associated with abandoned or unauthorized devices.

Scalability is a key consideration in mobile and IoT CIAM, as businesses must manage millions of user identities and device connections in real time. Cloud-based CIAM platforms provide scalable identity management services that handle high volumes of authentication requests without performance degradation. IoT environments, in particular, require scalable identity solutions that can support massive device networks while ensuring security and compliance.

By integrating CIAM with mobile and IoT strategies, businesses deliver secure, seamless, and user-friendly identity experiences across digital ecosystems. Strong authentication mechanisms, adaptive security controls, and privacy-centric identity management ensure that customers and devices can interact securely without compromising convenience. CIAM solutions tailored for mobile and IoT environments enable businesses to provide trusted digital experiences while protecting customer data and maintaining regulatory compliance.

The Future of Biometric Authentication

Biometric authentication is rapidly becoming the preferred method for identity verification, offering a secure and convenient alternative to traditional passwords. As technology evolves, biometrics are advancing beyond fingerprints and facial recognition to include voice, iris, gait, behavioral patterns, and even brainwave recognition. The growing adoption of biometric authentication across industries highlights its potential to enhance security, reduce fraud, and improve user experience while addressing emerging challenges related to privacy, ethics, and regulatory compliance.

The primary advantage of biometric authentication is its ability to provide secure, frictionless access without requiring users to remember complex passwords. Unlike passwords, which can be forgotten, stolen, or reused across multiple accounts, biometric identifiers are unique to each individual and difficult to replicate. Fingerprint and facial recognition are already widely used in smartphones, banking applications, and access control systems. However, advancements in artificial intelligence (AI) and machine learning (ML) are driving the development of more sophisticated biometric technologies that improve accuracy, security, and adaptability.

One of the key trends shaping the future of biometric authentication is multimodal biometrics, which combines multiple biometric factors for enhanced security and reliability. For example, a system may require both facial recognition and voice authentication to verify a user's identity. This approach mitigates the risk of spoofing attacks and enhances security by ensuring that authentication remains robust even if one biometric factor is compromised. Multimodal biometrics also improve accessibility, allowing users to authenticate through different modalities depending on their environment or physical abilities.

Behavioral biometrics is an emerging field that analyzes unique patterns in how individuals interact with devices and systems. Instead of relying on static biometric identifiers, behavioral biometrics continuously monitors characteristics such as typing speed, touchscreen pressure, mouse movements, and even walking patterns to verify user identity. This continuous authentication model enhances security by detecting anomalies in real time, preventing unauthorized access even if credentials or traditional biometrics have been compromised.

Advancements in AI-driven biometric authentication are also enabling more sophisticated anti-spoofing techniques. Presentation attacks, where fraudsters use photos, videos, or 3D masks to bypass biometric systems, pose a growing threat to facial recognition security. AI-powered liveness detection counters these attacks by analyzing subtle cues such as eye movement, skin texture, and depth perception to determine whether the presented biometric data is from a live person. These techniques improve the resilience of biometric authentication against fraud and identity theft.

Voice biometrics is gaining traction as a secure authentication method, particularly for call centers, banking applications, and virtual assistants. A user's voice contains unique characteristics such as pitch, tone, and pronunciation, making it a viable biometric identifier. AI-powered voice authentication can analyze voiceprints in real-time, enabling secure, hands-free authentication. However, challenges such as background noise, voice changes due to illness, and deepfake audio manipulation require continuous advancements in voice recognition algorithms to maintain accuracy and reliability.

Iris and retinal scanning offer high levels of security and accuracy due to the uniqueness of eye structures. These biometric methods are widely used in border control, law enforcement, and high-security environments. As sensor technology becomes more affordable and compact, iris recognition is expected to be integrated into consumer devices, offering a reliable alternative to fingerprint and facial recognition. The adoption of wearable biometric devices, such as smart glasses and augmented reality (AR) headsets, may further expand the use of iris authentication in daily interactions.

Gait recognition, which analyzes the way a person walks, is an emerging biometric technology with applications in surveillance, healthcare, and security. Unlike traditional biometrics that require direct user interaction, gait recognition can authenticate individuals from a distance. This technology is particularly useful for non-intrusive identity verification in public spaces, enhancing security while maintaining user convenience. However, challenges such as variations in walking patterns due to injuries or environmental conditions must be addressed to improve accuracy and reliability.

Brainwave authentication, also known as electroencephalography (EEG) biometrics, represents the cutting edge of identity verification. Research indicates that each individual has a unique brainwave pattern, which can be used as a biometric identifier. EEG-based authentication has potential applications in high-security environments, medical devices, and human-computer interaction. Although still in the experimental stage, brainwave biometrics could revolutionize authentication by providing an inherently unique and difficult-to-replicate security measure.

The widespread adoption of biometric authentication raises important privacy and ethical considerations. Unlike passwords, biometric data cannot be changed if compromised. A stolen fingerprint or facial scan could lead to irreversible security risks. To mitigate these concerns, businesses and technology providers must implement strong encryption, decentralized storage, and privacy-preserving techniques such as biometric template protection. Federated learning and homomorphic encryption are emerging as solutions that enable biometric authentication without exposing raw biometric data to centralized databases, reducing the risk of data breaches.

Regulatory compliance is another critical factor shaping the future of biometric authentication. Governments and regulatory bodies are establishing legal frameworks to govern the collection, storage, and use of biometric data. Regulations such as the General Data Protection Regulation (GDPR) and the California Consumer Privacy Act (CCPA) impose strict guidelines on biometric data handling, requiring businesses to obtain explicit user consent and implement data protection measures. Compliance with these regulations is essential to ensure that biometric authentication remains secure and ethically responsible.

The integration of biometric authentication with blockchain technology is an area of growing interest. Decentralized identity systems leverage blockchain to store encrypted biometric identifiers, allowing users to control access to their biometric data without relying on centralized authorities. This approach enhances privacy, reduces the risk of data breaches, and enables secure cross-platform authentication. Blockchain-based biometric identity solutions have potential applications in digital identity verification, border control, and secure online transactions.

As biometric authentication continues to evolve, businesses must adopt best practices to ensure security, usability, and compliance. A layered approach to authentication, combining biometrics with risk-based security measures and adaptive authentication, enhances protection while maintaining user convenience. Continuous innovation in AI-driven biometric recognition, anti-spoofing techniques, and decentralized identity frameworks will shape the future of biometric authentication, making it more secure, efficient, and accessible across industries.

Decentralized Identity and Blockchain in CIAM

Decentralized identity and blockchain technology are transforming Customer Identity and Access Management (CIAM) by providing users with greater control over their digital identities. Traditional CIAM solutions rely on centralized databases and identity providers to store and manage customer credentials, creating security risks and privacy concerns. Decentralized identity shifts control from organizations to individuals, allowing them to own, manage, and share their credentials securely without depending on third-party intermediaries. Blockchain technology enables this model by providing a tamper-proof and transparent ledger for verifying identity attributes while maintaining user privacy.

The core principle of decentralized identity is self-sovereign identity (SSI), which gives individuals full ownership over their identity information. Instead of relying on service providers to authenticate users, decentralized identity allows customers to store their credentials in secure digital wallets and present verifiable identity proofs only when necessary. This approach reduces reliance on centralized identity repositories, which are often targets for cyberattacks, and minimizes the risk of identity theft, data breaches, and unauthorized access.

Blockchain technology plays a crucial role in enabling decentralized identity by providing a secure and immutable ledger for storing and verifying identity claims. Unlike traditional identity management systems that store personal data on centralized servers, blockchain based CIAM solutions use cryptographic methods to issue and verify digital credentials without exposing sensitive information. Each user's identity attributes are stored as verifiable credentials, which can be cryptographically signed by trusted issuers and shared selectively with service providers.

One of the most significant advantages of decentralized identity in CIAM is enhanced privacy. Traditional authentication methods often require users to disclose excessive personal information to access services. With decentralized identity, users can share only the necessary identity attributes while maintaining control over their data.

For example, instead of providing a full government-issued ID for age verification, a user can present a verifiable credential that confirms they are above the required age without revealing their date of birth. This selective disclosure capability strengthens privacy and minimizes the exposure of personal information.

Verifiable credentials are a key component of decentralized identity, enabling users to prove their identity without relying on centralized authorities. These credentials are issued by trusted entities such as government agencies, financial institutions, or educational organizations and stored in a user-controlled digital wallet. When users need to authenticate themselves, they can present a cryptographic proof derived from their verifiable credentials, which can be verified instantly using blockchain-based decentralized identifiers (DIDs). This eliminates the need for passwords and reduces the risk of phishing attacks and credential theft.

Decentralized identity also enhances security by reducing the attack surface associated with centralized identity management. In traditional CIAM models, databases storing customer credentials are attractive targets for hackers seeking to compromise large volumes of sensitive data. By removing the need for centralized identity storage, decentralized identity eliminates single points of failure, making it significantly more difficult for cybercriminals to access user information. Blockchain's immutable nature ensures that identity records cannot be altered or forged, providing an additional layer of security against fraud and identity manipulation.

Interoperability is a critical factor in the adoption of decentralized identity solutions within CIAM. Businesses and organizations operate across multiple platforms, requiring a seamless authentication experience that works across different systems. Standards such as the World Wide Web Consortium's (W3C) Decentralized Identifiers (DIDs) and Verifiable Credentials (VCs) frameworks ensure that decentralized identity solutions remain compatible with existing digital identity ecosystems. These standards enable users to authenticate themselves across various applications, industries, and service providers without creating multiple accounts or sharing unnecessary personal information.

Decentralized identity is particularly beneficial for industries that require strong identity verification, such as finance, healthcare, and government services. In the financial sector, blockchain-based identity solutions can streamline Know Your Customer (KYC) compliance by enabling financial institutions to verify customer identities without requiring repeated data submissions. Healthcare providers can leverage decentralized identity to give patients secure access to medical records while ensuring compliance with data protection regulations such as the Health Insurance Portability and Accountability Act (HIPAA). Government agencies can issue digital identity credentials that citizens can use for secure online interactions, reducing reliance on paper-based documentation.

One of the challenges in implementing decentralized identity within CIAM is ensuring user adoption and ease of use. While blockchain technology provides strong security guarantees, the complexity of managing cryptographic keys and digital wallets may be a barrier for non-technical users. User-friendly interfaces, automated key recovery mechanisms, and integration with existing authentication methods can help bridge the gap between decentralized identity and mainstream adoption. Businesses adopting decentralized identity must ensure that the user experience remains intuitive while maintaining high levels of security.

Regulatory compliance and legal considerations also impact the adoption of decentralized identity. Data protection laws such as the General Data Protection Regulation (GDPR) and the California Consumer Privacy Act (CCPA) impose strict requirements on how organizations collect, store, and process personal data. Decentralized identity aligns with these regulations by giving users full control over their personal information and reducing the need for organizations to store sensitive data. However, legal frameworks must continue evolving to accommodate decentralized identity models and address concerns related to accountability, liability, and governance.

Another important aspect of decentralized identity in CIAM is trust management. While blockchain ensures data integrity, the trustworthiness of identity issuers remains a key consideration. Businesses and users must rely on trusted identity providers to issue verifiable credentials that can be accepted across different platforms.

Decentralized trust frameworks, such as identity verification consortia and reputation-based models, can help establish a network of trusted issuers, ensuring that identity claims are valid and universally recognized.

The integration of decentralized identity with Internet of Things (IoT) devices presents additional opportunities for CIAM. IoT ecosystems require secure identity authentication to prevent unauthorized access to connected devices and networks. Decentralized identity allows IoT devices to register themselves with blockchain-based identifiers, ensuring that only authorized devices can interact within secure environments. This capability enhances IoT security by eliminating reliance on weak password-based authentication methods and providing a scalable identity solution for smart cities, industrial IoT, and connected healthcare systems.

As decentralized identity continues to gain traction, businesses must evaluate how to integrate blockchain-based identity solutions into their CIAM strategies. Hybrid identity models that combine traditional authentication methods with decentralized identity principles can provide a gradual transition toward decentralized identity adoption. Organizations that embrace decentralized identity will benefit from enhanced security, improved privacy, and reduced dependency on centralized identity providers, ultimately shaping the future of digital identity management.

Zero Trust and CIAM Alignment

Zero Trust is a modern security framework that eliminates the traditional notion of a trusted network perimeter and assumes that every access request must be verified, regardless of its origin. In an era of increasing cyber threats, remote work, and digital transformation, organizations can no longer rely on static security models that trust internal users by default. Instead, Zero Trust requires continuous authentication, least privilege access, and contextual risk assessment. Customer Identity and Access Management (CIAM) plays a crucial role in aligning with the Zero Trust model by ensuring secure authentication, adaptive access control, and identity-centric security measures.

At the core of Zero Trust is the principle of "never trust, always verify." Unlike traditional security models that grant implicit trust to users and devices within a corporate network, Zero Trust continuously evaluates every request based on identity, device health, location, and behavioral patterns. CIAM enhances this approach by providing strong authentication mechanisms, identity verification, and adaptive security measures that help organizations enforce Zero Trust principles while delivering seamless user experiences.

A fundamental aspect of Zero Trust and CIAM alignment is identity-centric security. Instead of relying on network-based security controls, Zero Trust shifts the focus to verifying users and devices at every interaction. CIAM platforms provide robust identity verification methods, including multi-factor authentication (MFA), biometric authentication, and passwordless login. These methods ensure that only legitimate users gain access to digital services, reducing the risk of credential-based attacks such as phishing and account takeovers.

Adaptive authentication is a critical component in enforcing Zero Trust security policies. CIAM solutions use risk-based authentication (RBA) to analyze contextual factors such as device type, IP reputation, geographic location, and user behavior before granting access. If a login attempt appears risky—such as an access request from an unfamiliar device or an unusual location—the system may enforce step-up authentication, requiring additional verification before access is granted. This dynamic approach aligns with Zero Trust by ensuring that authentication is not a one-time event but an ongoing process that adapts to risk levels in real time.

The principle of least privilege is another key element of Zero Trust that aligns with CIAM access control policies. Instead of granting broad access permissions, users should only receive the minimum level of access required to perform specific actions. CIAM solutions enforce fine-grained access control through role-based access control (RBAC) and attribute-based access control (ABAC). RBAC assigns permissions based on predefined roles, ensuring that customers, partners, and employees only access relevant resources. ABAC takes a more granular approach by evaluating dynamic attributes such as user role, session context, and transaction type before granting access.

Continuous authentication further strengthens Zero Trust security by verifying user identities throughout their sessions. Traditional authentication methods only validate users at login, leaving sessions vulnerable to hijacking or unauthorized access. CIAM platforms integrate continuous authentication mechanisms that monitor user activity, device behavior, and session anomalies to detect suspicious patterns. If an active session deviates from normal behavior—such as a sudden change in location or unusual transaction activity—the system can require reauthentication, restrict actions, or terminate the session altogether.

Zero Trust also emphasizes device security and endpoint verification, ensuring that only trusted devices can access sensitive applications and services. CIAM solutions incorporate device intelligence and endpoint security checks to assess whether a device is compliant with security policies before granting access. This includes evaluating device fingerprinting, software version updates, and malware detection to prevent compromised endpoints from accessing critical resources. Organizations can integrate CIAM with endpoint detection and response (EDR) systems to enforce security policies dynamically based on device health and risk posture.

API security is another area where CIAM and Zero Trust principles align. As organizations increasingly rely on APIs for customer interactions, securing API access becomes a priority. CIAM platforms enforce API authentication and authorization using industry standards such as OAuth 2.0 and OpenID Connect (OIDC). These protocols ensure that only authenticated users and applications can access APIs, reducing the risk of unauthorized data exposure. Zero Trust API security also includes rate limiting, anomaly detection, and token-based authentication to prevent API abuse and mitigate threats such as credential stuffing and API scraping.

Zero Trust requires comprehensive logging, monitoring, and auditing to detect and respond to security incidents. CIAM solutions integrate with Security Information and Event Management (SIEM) platforms to provide real-time visibility into authentication attempts, access requests, and user behavior anomalies. By continuously analyzing identity-related events, organizations can detect suspicious activities, enforce security policies, and respond to threats before they escalate. AI-driven analytics further enhance this process by identifying patterns of compromised accounts, brute-force attempts, and insider threats.

Compliance and regulatory requirements also play a significant role in the alignment between Zero Trust and CIAM. Data protection regulations such as the General Data Protection Regulation (GDPR), California Consumer Privacy Act (CCPA), and Payment Card Industry Data Security Standard (PCI DSS) mandate strong identity security measures to protect customer data. CIAM enables organizations to meet these compliance standards by enforcing strong authentication, consent management, and access control policies. Zero Trust frameworks support compliance by implementing continuous risk assessment and identity-based security controls that align with regulatory guidelines.

Zero Trust and CIAM integration extend beyond traditional IT environments to support cloud-based applications, hybrid infrastructures, and multi-cloud deployments. As organizations migrate workloads to the cloud, ensuring secure access across diverse environments becomes essential. CIAM platforms facilitate cloud identity federation, enabling seamless authentication across cloud service providers while enforcing Zero Trust access policies. Identity-as-a-Service (IDaaS) solutions provide centralized identity management, reducing complexity and improving security across cloud ecosystems.

Organizations implementing Zero Trust and CIAM strategies must prioritize user experience while maintaining strong security. Excessive authentication challenges can frustrate users and lead to account abandonment. CIAM solutions balance security and usability by offering adaptive authentication, biometric login options, and federated identity management. By reducing friction in authentication processes, businesses can enhance customer trust while maintaining Zero Trust security standards.

The alignment between Zero Trust and CIAM is essential for protecting digital identities, preventing unauthorized access, and securing modern IT ecosystems. By enforcing continuous authentication, least privilege access, adaptive security measures, and API protection, businesses can create a resilient identity-centric security framework. As cyber threats continue to evolve, integrating Zero Trust principles into CIAM ensures that organizations remain proactive in safeguarding customer identities while delivering secure and seamless digital experiences.

The Role of CIAM in B2C, B2B, and B2E

Customer Identity and Access Management (CIAM) serves as a foundational component in digital identity management, addressing authentication, authorization, and user experience across different business models. Whether an organization operates in a Business-to-Consumer (B2C), Business-to-Business (B2B), or Business-to-Employee (B2E) environment, CIAM solutions play a critical role in securing access, managing user identities, and ensuring compliance with security and privacy regulations. Each business model presents unique identity management challenges that require tailored CIAM implementations to optimize user interactions, security controls, and operational efficiency.

In a B2C environment, CIAM is primarily focused on delivering seamless and secure experiences for customers who interact with digital services. Consumers expect fast and frictionless authentication processes, personalized interactions, and the ability to manage their own accounts effortlessly. CIAM solutions in B2C prioritize user convenience while ensuring strong security measures to protect against fraud, identity theft, and account takeovers.

One of the key aspects of CIAM in B2C is scalable authentication. Businesses serving large consumer bases must handle millions of authentication requests daily without causing performance degradation. Cloud-based CIAM solutions enable organizations to scale authentication services dynamically, ensuring that peak traffic events—such as sales promotions, seasonal spikes, or product launches—do not disrupt the user experience.

Social login is a common feature in B2C CIAM implementations, allowing users to authenticate using existing credentials from identity providers such as Google, Apple, or Facebook. This eliminates the need for customers to create and remember new passwords, reducing friction in the registration process and increasing conversion rates. CIAM also supports progressive profiling, enabling businesses to collect user data incrementally over time rather than requiring extensive information upfront, which can deter new users from completing registration.

Security remains a top priority in B2C CIAM, with multi-factor authentication (MFA), risk-based authentication (RBA), and biometric authentication playing essential roles in safeguarding customer identities. Adaptive authentication assesses contextual factors—such as device type, location, and login behavior—to determine whether additional security measures are necessary. This ensures that legitimate users can access their accounts with minimal friction while preventing fraudulent access attempts.

In a B2B environment, CIAM extends beyond customer interactions to facilitate secure and controlled access for business partners, suppliers, and enterprise customers. Unlike B2C, where identity management focuses on individual users, B2B CIAM must accommodate organizations with multiple users, varying access levels, and complex authorization structures.

Federated identity management is a critical feature in B2B CIAM, enabling organizations to authenticate users across multiple systems and partner networks without requiring separate login credentials for each platform. Businesses often integrate CIAM with Single Sign-On (SSO) solutions to streamline authentication and authorization across enterprise applications, reducing login friction and improving security. SSO ensures that users can access multiple systems with a single authentication event, enhancing productivity while minimizing the risk of credential-related security breaches.

Granular access control is essential in B2B CIAM, as businesses must enforce strict authorization policies to prevent unauthorized access to sensitive data and corporate resources. Role-based access control (RBAC) and attribute-based access control (ABAC) allow organizations to define user permissions based on roles, responsibilities, and contextual factors. This ensures that users only have access to the information and applications relevant to their business function.

API security is another key consideration in B2B CIAM, as businesses increasingly rely on API-driven integrations to connect with partners and enterprise customers. OAuth 2.0 and OpenID Connect (OIDC) provide secure authentication and authorization for API-based interactions, ensuring that external entities can access business services without exposing sensitive credentials. API security mechanisms such as rate limiting, anomaly detection, and token-based authentication further enhance the security posture of B2B environments.

CIAM in a B2E context focuses on managing employee identities, ensuring secure access to internal systems, and enabling workforce productivity. Unlike B2C and B2B, where external users interact with business applications, B2E CIAM is designed for internal users, including employees, contractors, and temporary workers.

Strong identity governance is a core component of B2E CIAM, ensuring that employees receive appropriate access permissions while minimizing security risks. Identity lifecycle management automates user provisioning and deprovisioning, ensuring that employees gain access to necessary systems upon onboarding and lose access immediately upon termination or role changes. This prevents unauthorized access and reduces the risk of insider threats.

B2E CIAM also incorporates Zero Trust security principles, which require continuous verification of user identities and device security before granting access to corporate resources. Unlike traditional perimeter-based security models, Zero Trust assumes that no user or device should be trusted by default. Continuous authentication, endpoint security checks, and risk-based access controls ensure that employees access corporate systems securely, whether working from the office, remotely, or on personal devices.

Biometric authentication and passwordless login methods enhance security and user experience in B2E environments. Employees can authenticate using fingerprint scans, facial recognition, or hardware security keys instead of relying on traditional passwords. These authentication methods reduce the risk of credential-based attacks, improve login efficiency, and enhance overall security.

Compliance with industry regulations and data protection laws is a key driver of CIAM adoption in all three business models. B2C organizations must comply with regulations such as the General Data Protection Regulation (GDPR) and the California Consumer Privacy Act (CCPA), ensuring that customer data is handled securely and transparently. B2B companies must adhere to contractual security requirements and industry-specific regulations, such as the Payment Card Industry Data Security Standard (PCI DSS) for financial transactions. B2E CIAM must meet corporate compliance mandates such as the Health Insurance Portability and Accountability Act (HIPAA) for healthcare data security and the Sarbanes-Oxley Act (SOX) for corporate governance.

The integration of CIAM across B2C, B2B, and B2E environments enables businesses to deliver secure, efficient, and personalized digital experiences. While each business model presents unique identity management challenges, CIAM solutions provide the necessary tools to enforce authentication policies, manage user identities, and maintain compliance with evolving security and privacy standards. By leveraging CIAM effectively, organizations strengthen security, enhance user trust, and streamline access management across diverse digital ecosystems.

CIAM for Financial Services and Banking

Customer Identity and Access Management (CIAM) plays a vital role in financial services and banking, where security, compliance, and user experience must be carefully balanced. Banks and financial institutions handle sensitive customer data, process high-value transactions, and operate under strict regulatory frameworks, making robust identity management essential. A well-implemented CIAM solution enhances security, prevents fraud, and delivers seamless digital experiences while ensuring compliance with financial regulations.

One of the key challenges in financial services is protecting customer identities against fraud and unauthorized access. Cybercriminals frequently target financial institutions using phishing attacks, credential stuffing, account takeovers, and identity theft. Traditional authentication methods, such as passwords, are no longer sufficient to safeguard customer accounts. CIAM solutions integrate strong authentication mechanisms, including multi-factor authentication (MFA), biometric authentication, and passwordless login, to reduce the risk of credential-based attacks.

Adaptive authentication is particularly valuable in banking CIAM, as it assesses contextual factors to determine authentication requirements dynamically. Instead of applying the same security measures to all users, adaptive authentication evaluates factors such as device reputation, login location, behavioral biometrics, and transaction risk before granting access. If an authentication attempt appears suspicious, step-up authentication measures, such as requiring additional verification via SMS, email, or a mobile authenticator app, are triggered to confirm the user's identity.

Fraud detection and prevention are critical components of CIAM for financial institutions. Advanced CIAM platforms leverage artificial intelligence (AI) and machine learning (ML) to analyze authentication patterns, transaction behaviors, and risk signals in real time. By detecting anomalies—such as sudden large withdrawals, multiple login attempts from different locations, or unusual transaction activity—CIAM systems can automatically block fraudulent activities or require further verification before processing transactions. AI-driven identity verification helps banks detect and prevent fraudulent account openings, synthetic identities, and financial fraud attempts.

Regulatory compliance is a major driver of CIAM adoption in financial services. Banks and financial institutions must comply with data protection laws, financial security regulations, and anti-money laundering (AML) directives. Regulations such as the General Data Protection Regulation (GDPR), the California Consumer Privacy Act (CCPA), and the Payment Card Industry Data Security Standard (PCI DSS) require financial organizations to protect customer data, enforce strong authentication measures, and implement transparent consent management. Additionally, regulations like the Revised Payment Services Directive (PSD2) in Europe mandate strong customer authentication (SCA) for online transactions, requiring CIAM solutions to support secure identity verification processes.

A seamless onboarding experience is essential for financial institutions, as lengthy or complex registration processes can lead to customer drop-offs. CIAM solutions streamline digital onboarding by integrating electronic Know Your Customer (eKYC) verification, document scanning, and biometric authentication. Instead of requiring customers to visit physical bank branches for identity verification, banks can use CIAM to enable remote onboarding with facial recognition, ID verification, and real-time database checks. This reduces friction while ensuring compliance with identity verification regulations.

CIAM also enables secure account recovery and self-service account management in banking applications. Customers frequently forget passwords, lose access to authentication devices, or need to update personal details. Secure self-service options allow users to reset passwords, change authentication preferences, and update contact information without requiring manual intervention from bank representatives. Secure recovery mechanisms, such as identity verification via biometrics or registered email accounts, prevent unauthorized access while enhancing customer convenience.

Omnichannel banking experiences rely on CIAM to provide consistent and secure authentication across multiple platforms, including web banking portals, mobile banking apps, ATMs, and call centers. Customers expect to access their accounts seamlessly across different devices without repeated authentication friction. CIAM solutions enable Single Sign-On (SSO) across banking services, ensuring that customers can authenticate once and securely access multiple banking applications without the need for redundant logins. Secure session management ensures that authenticated users can navigate between banking services while maintaining session integrity and security.

Financial institutions must also manage consent and data privacy effectively. Customers need control over how their personal and financial data is collected, shared, and processed. CIAM platforms include consent management tools that allow users to review, modify, or revoke consent for data sharing, ensuring compliance with privacy regulations. Open banking initiatives, such as PSD2, require banks to provide third-party service providers (TPPs) with secure access to customer data upon user consent. CIAM enables secure API authentication and authorization, ensuring that only authorized TPPs can access customer information while protecting sensitive financial data.

Biometric authentication is becoming a standard in banking CIAM, providing a secure and frictionless authentication experience. Banks integrate fingerprint scanning, facial recognition, and voice authentication to enable secure access to mobile banking apps and ATM transactions. Biometric authentication enhances security by eliminating password-related vulnerabilities while improving customer convenience. Continuous authentication mechanisms, such as behavioral biometrics, further strengthen security by analyzing keystroke patterns, touchscreen gestures, and navigation behaviors to detect anomalies in real time.

Third-party identity federation allows financial institutions to streamline authentication processes by integrating with trusted identity providers. Many customers prefer to use existing digital identities, such as government-issued digital IDs or social login credentials, instead of creating new banking credentials. CIAM enables financial institutions to support federated authentication, allowing users to authenticate with verified identity providers while maintaining strong security controls.

Secure API access is a crucial component of CIAM in banking, ensuring that financial data and services are protected against unauthorized access. Banks rely on APIs to facilitate digital banking transactions, mobile payments, and third-party integrations. CIAM enforces OAuth 2.0 and OpenID Connect (OIDC) protocols to authenticate API requests securely, ensuring that only authorized applications and users can access banking services. API security measures, such as token-based authentication, rate limiting, and anomaly detection, help prevent API abuse, credential stuffing, and unauthorized transactions.

Risk-based transaction monitoring is another CIAM capability that enhances banking security. Instead of applying uniform security measures to all transactions, CIAM evaluates transaction risk levels based on user behavior, location, transaction history, and device trustworthiness. High-risk transactions, such as international fund transfers or large withdrawals, may require step-up authentication to verify user intent. Real-time fraud detection and automated response mechanisms help banks prevent unauthorized transactions while allowing legitimate users to complete low-risk operations seamlessly.

CIAM plays a pivotal role in securing financial ecosystems while delivering frictionless digital banking experiences. By integrating strong authentication mechanisms, adaptive security measures, and compliance-driven identity governance, financial institutions enhance customer trust, prevent fraud, and ensure regulatory compliance. The adoption of biometric authentication, AI-driven fraud detection, and secure API access further strengthens banking CIAM, enabling financial services to provide secure and user-friendly digital interactions.

CIAM for Retail and E-Commerce

Customer Identity and Access Management (CIAM) is essential for retail and e-commerce businesses looking to enhance customer experiences while maintaining strong security and compliance. As consumers demand personalized, seamless, and secure online shopping experiences, retailers must implement robust identity management strategies that facilitate effortless authentication, protect against fraud, and enable omnichannel interactions. A well-structured CIAM solution provides retailers with the tools to balance convenience and security while optimizing customer engagement.

One of the key drivers of CIAM in retail and e-commerce is the need for frictionless authentication. Customers expect to log in quickly, browse products, and complete transactions without unnecessary delays. Traditional username-password authentication can create frustration, leading to cart abandonment and reduced conversion rates. Retailers address this challenge by implementing passwordless authentication methods such as social login, biometric authentication, and Single Sign-On (SSO). Social login allows customers to use existing credentials from platforms like Google, Facebook, or Apple, eliminating the need to create new accounts. This simplifies registration while increasing conversion rates and reducing password-related issues.

Personalization is a critical component of modern retail experiences, and CIAM plays a crucial role in enabling customized interactions. Retailers collect customer data such as purchase history, browsing behavior, and preferences to deliver targeted recommendations, promotions, and loyalty rewards. CIAM solutions facilitate progressive profiling, allowing businesses to gather customer information gradually instead of requiring extensive details upfront. By collecting relevant data over time, retailers improve personalization while reducing registration friction.

Security remains a top priority for e-commerce businesses, as online retailers are frequent targets of fraud, account takeovers, and payment fraud. CIAM solutions enhance security by integrating multi-factor authentication (MFA), risk-based authentication, and adaptive security measures. Risk-based authentication evaluates contextual factors such as device type, location, and transaction value before determining authentication requirements. If a login attempt or transaction appears suspicious, step-up authentication—such as an OTP sent via SMS or biometric verification—is triggered to confirm the user's identity. This dynamic security approach prevents unauthorized access while minimizing friction for legitimate customers.

Omnichannel retailing relies on seamless identity management across multiple platforms, including websites, mobile apps, in-store kiosks, and customer service portals. CIAM ensures that customers can authenticate once and access all retail services without repeated logins. Whether a customer browses products on a mobile app, adds items to a cart on a desktop site, and completes the purchase in-store, CIAM enables a unified experience. Cross-channel identity synchronization ensures that shopping preferences, loyalty points, and personalized recommendations remain consistent across all touchpoints.

Loyalty programs are a major driver of customer retention in retail, and CIAM enables secure and personalized loyalty program management. Retailers use CIAM to verify customer identities when awarding or redeeming loyalty points, preventing fraud while ensuring a seamless experience. Customers should be able to log in once and access their rewards across different channels without needing to reauthenticate or enter multiple verification codes. A well-integrated CIAM system allows retailers to tailor loyalty offers based on customer behavior, increasing engagement and repeat purchases.

Fraud prevention is a major concern for e-commerce businesses, as cybercriminals target online transactions using stolen credentials, credit card fraud, and automated bot attacks. CIAM solutions integrate AI-driven fraud detection to analyze transaction patterns, detect anomalies, and prevent fraudulent activities in real time. Behavioral biometrics further enhance fraud prevention by monitoring how users interact with a website or mobile app—such as keystroke dynamics, mouse movements, and touchscreen gestures. If a login attempt or transaction deviates from normal behavior, the system can trigger additional verification steps or block the transaction entirely.

Secure API access is another critical aspect of CIAM in retail and e-commerce. Many retailers operate on interconnected platforms, leveraging third party services for payment processing, inventory management, and order fulfillment. CIAM solutions enforce secure API authentication using OAuth 2.0 and OpenID Connect (OIDC), ensuring that only authorized applications and services can access customer data. API security measures, such as token-based authentication, rate limiting, and anomaly detection, protect against API abuse and data breaches.

Compliance with data protection regulations is essential for retailers handling customer identity and payment information. Regulations such as the General Data Protection Regulation (GDPR), the California Consumer Privacy Act (CCPA), and the Payment Card Industry Data

Security Standard (PCI DSS) require businesses to implement strong security controls and provide customers with transparency regarding data collection and processing. CIAM solutions include consent management tools that allow customers to review, modify, or revoke consent for data usage. This ensures compliance with privacy regulations while fostering trust with customers.

Seamless checkout experiences are a key factor in reducing cart abandonment and increasing conversions. CIAM solutions enable secure and user-friendly checkout processes by integrating one-click authentication, biometric payment confirmation, and stored payment credentials. Customers who authenticate using a CIAM-enabled digital wallet can complete purchases without manually entering payment details, reducing friction while maintaining strong security controls.

Mobile commerce is rapidly growing, and CIAM enhances security and usability for mobile shoppers. Mobile CIAM implementations include biometric login, device authentication, and push notification authentication to provide a frictionless experience. Secure mobile authentication methods eliminate reliance on passwords, reducing the risk of account takeovers while streamlining the shopping process.

Retailers leveraging CIAM also gain valuable insights into customer behavior, enabling data-driven decision-making. Analytics tools integrated with CIAM provide insights into login trends, authentication success rates, and fraud detection patterns. Businesses can use this data to optimize marketing campaigns, improve user experience, and enhance security policies. By analyzing authentication data, retailers can identify high-risk transactions, adjust security policies dynamically, and tailor personalized experiences based on customer engagement.

Retail and e-commerce businesses must ensure that their CIAM strategies align with evolving consumer expectations, security threats, and regulatory requirements. By implementing strong authentication measures, seamless omnichannel identity management, and AI-driven fraud prevention, retailers can provide secure and frictionless customer experiences. CIAM not only protects against security risks but also enhances customer engagement, personalization, and loyalty, making it a critical component of modern retail and e-commerce success.

CIAM for Healthcare and Telemedicine

Customer Identity and Access Management (CIAM) plays a critical role in healthcare and telemedicine by securing patient identities, protecting sensitive medical data, and ensuring seamless access to digital health services. As the healthcare industry continues to shift toward digital platforms, electronic health records (EHRs), and virtual consultations, robust identity management becomes essential. Patients, healthcare providers, and administrators require secure yet user-friendly authentication methods that comply with strict regulatory requirements while maintaining accessibility and privacy.

One of the most significant challenges in healthcare CIAM is balancing security with ease of access. Patients need quick and seamless access to their medical records, appointment scheduling, and telehealth services without encountering authentication barriers that might deter them from using digital healthcare platforms. At the same time, healthcare organizations must protect sensitive patient information from unauthorized access, data breaches, and identity fraud. CIAM solutions address this challenge by implementing strong authentication mechanisms, including multi-factor authentication (MFA), biometric authentication, and adaptive access controls.

MFA enhances security by requiring users to verify their identity using two or more factors, such as a password combined with a fingerprint scan or a one-time passcode (OTP) sent via SMS or email. While MFA strengthens protection against unauthorized access, it must be implemented in a way that does not create unnecessary friction for patients, especially those who may have limited technical expertise. Adaptive authentication helps streamline this process by analyzing risk factors—such as device type, login location, and behavioral patterns— to determine when additional verification is necessary. Patients logging in from a trusted device and location can be granted access with minimal friction, while high-risk login attempts may trigger step-up authentication.

Telemedicine platforms rely on CIAM to authenticate patients and healthcare providers securely. Virtual consultations require identity verification to ensure that medical professionals and patients are who they claim to be. CIAM enables healthcare organizations to implement secure video conferencing authentication, ensuring that only authorized participants can access telehealth sessions. Biometric authentication, such as facial recognition or fingerprint scanning, provides a frictionless yet secure method of verifying patient identities before a consultation begins.

Regulatory compliance is a crucial aspect of CIAM in healthcare. Laws such as the Health Insurance Portability and Accountability Act (HIPAA) in the United States, the General Data Protection Regulation (GDPR) in Europe, and other regional data protection laws mandate strict security and privacy controls for patient data. CIAM solutions facilitate compliance by implementing role-based access control (RBAC), consent management, and audit logging. RBAC ensures that only authorized personnel—such as doctors, nurses, and administrators—can access specific patient records based on their roles. Consent management features allow patients to control how their medical data is shared, ensuring transparency and adherence to data protection regulations.

Interoperability is another critical factor in healthcare identity management. Patients often receive care from multiple providers, requiring secure identity verification across different healthcare systems, hospitals, and pharmacies. CIAM solutions enable federated identity management, allowing patients to use a single set of credentials across multiple healthcare platforms. Identity federation supports Single Sign-On (SSO), ensuring that patients and providers can access interconnected healthcare services without needing to log in multiple times.

Secure access to electronic health records (EHRs) is a major use case for CIAM in healthcare. Patients should be able to view their medical history, lab results, prescriptions, and treatment plans securely through patient portals and mobile health applications. CIAM solutions implement secure API authentication to protect EHR access, ensuring that only authorized users can retrieve sensitive medical data. OAuth 2.0 and OpenID Connect (OIDC) enable secure identity verification for EHR access, allowing healthcare providers and third-party applications to retrieve medical information while ensuring data privacy.

The rise of remote patient monitoring (RPM) and connected healthcare devices further increases the importance of CIAM. Wearables, smart medical devices, and home monitoring systems generate continuous health data that needs to be securely linked to a patient's identity. CIAM enables secure device authentication, ensuring that only authorized medical devices can transmit data to healthcare systems. By implementing device identity management, healthcare providers can prevent unauthorized devices from accessing patient data, reducing the risk of cyber threats and data tampering.

Fraud prevention is another essential aspect of CIAM in healthcare. Identity fraud can have severe consequences in medical settings, including insurance fraud, prescription drug fraud, and unauthorized access to patient records. CIAM solutions incorporate AI-driven fraud detection to analyze authentication patterns, detect anomalies, and prevent identity-based fraud. Behavioral biometrics, such as keystroke dynamics and navigation patterns, help differentiate between legitimate users and fraudulent attempts, enhancing security without disrupting patient access.

Healthcare organizations must also provide secure self-service account management for patients. Patients should be able to update personal information, manage authentication preferences, and review access logs without requiring manual intervention from healthcare administrators. CIAM solutions integrate self-service portals that allow users to reset passwords, change authentication methods, and modify privacy preferences in compliance with healthcare regulations. This not only enhances user convenience but also reduces the administrative burden on healthcare IT teams.

Patient trust is a cornerstone of digital healthcare, and CIAM plays a vital role in fostering that trust. Transparent identity management practices, clear consent policies, and strong security controls reassure patients that their medical data is protected. Privacy-by-design principles embedded within CIAM solutions ensure that patient identities are safeguarded from unauthorized access, data breaches, and identity misuse.

Scalability is a crucial consideration for healthcare CIAM implementations. Hospitals, clinics, and telemedicine providers must accommodate millions of patients while maintaining high-performance authentication and identity verification processes. Cloud-based CIAM platforms provide scalable identity management, ensuring that authentication services remain responsive during peak usage periods, such as public health emergencies or vaccine rollouts.

As the healthcare industry continues to embrace digital transformation, CIAM will remain a fundamental component of securing patient identities, enabling seamless access to medical services, and ensuring regulatory compliance. By integrating strong authentication methods, adaptive security measures, and interoperable identity management, healthcare organizations can provide secure, efficient, and patient-centric digital experiences while protecting sensitive medical information.

CIAM Implementation Best Practices

Implementing a robust Customer Identity and Access Management (CIAM) solution requires a strategic approach to ensure security, usability, scalability, and compliance. As businesses increasingly rely on digital platforms to engage with customers, CIAM plays a critical role in providing seamless authentication, protecting sensitive data, and improving user experience. A well-executed CIAM strategy enhances security while minimizing friction, ensuring that customers can access services securely and efficiently.

One of the foundational best practices in CIAM implementation is adopting a user-centric approach. Customers expect simple and frictionless authentication processes that do not require unnecessary steps. Complicated registration and login procedures often lead to abandonment, negatively impacting engagement and conversions.

Offering social login, passwordless authentication, and Single Sign-On (SSO) can streamline user access and improve convenience. Progressive profiling, which collects user data gradually rather than requiring extensive details at registration, further enhances the user experience while ensuring businesses gather relevant identity information over time.

Security remains a top priority in CIAM, and implementing multi-factor authentication (MFA) is essential to mitigating identity fraud and unauthorized access. While MFA adds an extra layer of security, it should be implemented intelligently to minimize friction for legitimate users. Adaptive authentication analyzes contextual factors such as device type, geolocation, login history, and behavioral patterns to determine when step-up authentication is necessary. If an authentication attempt is deemed low-risk, the system can allow access with minimal verification, whereas high-risk attempts trigger additional authentication steps.

Ensuring strong password policies is another critical best practice, although passwordless authentication is becoming the preferred alternative. If passwords are still required, organizations should enforce policies that prevent weak or commonly used passwords and encourage the use of password managers. Passwordless authentication methods, such as biometric authentication, magic links, and one-time passcodes (OTPs), enhance security while eliminating the risks associated with stolen or reused passwords.

Scalability is an essential factor in CIAM implementation, especially for businesses that experience fluctuating user demand. E-commerce platforms, financial institutions, and streaming services often see spikes in traffic during sales events, holidays, or promotional campaigns. A cloud-based CIAM solution with elastic scalability ensures that authentication services remain responsive even during peak loads. Organizations should choose a CIAM platform that can handle millions of authentication requests simultaneously without performance degradation.

Privacy and regulatory compliance are integral to a successful CIAM strategy. With data protection regulations such as the General Data Protection Regulation (GDPR), the California Consumer Privacy Act

(CCPA), and industry-specific standards like the Payment Card Industry Data Security Standard (PCI DSS), organizations must ensure that customer identities and personal data are handled securely. CIAM solutions should include built-in consent management, allowing users to control how their data is used and providing transparent privacy policies. Businesses should also implement data minimization principles, collecting only the necessary information required for authentication and service personalization.

Secure API access is another best practice in CIAM implementation, as modern digital ecosystems rely on APIs to enable authentication, identity verification, and user data management. OAuth 2.0 and OpenID Connect (OIDC) are widely adopted standards that ensure secure API-based authentication and authorization. Organizations should enforce token-based authentication, implement API rate limiting, and continuously monitor API activity to detect and prevent security threats such as credential stuffing and unauthorized data access.

CIAM implementation should include identity federation capabilities to enable seamless authentication across multiple platforms and services. Organizations operating in multi-brand, partner, or franchise environments benefit from federated identity, which allows customers to authenticate once and access multiple digital properties without creating separate accounts. Identity federation also supports integration with third-party identity providers, enabling users to authenticate using existing credentials from providers such as Google, Facebook, or Microsoft.

Fraud prevention measures must be integrated into CIAM to detect and mitigate account takeover attempts, fake account creation, and identity theft. Artificial intelligence (AI) and machine learning (ML) can analyze authentication patterns, detect anomalies, and prevent fraudulent activities in real time. Behavioral biometrics further strengthen fraud detection by assessing user interaction patterns, such as typing speed, mouse movements, and touchscreen gestures. Implementing these techniques ensures that businesses can differentiate between legitimate users and malicious actors without disrupting the user experience.

Seamless integration with customer relationship management (CRM) and marketing platforms enhances personalization and engagement. CIAM solutions should synchronize user identities with business applications to enable personalized recommendations, targeted promotions, and loyalty program management. By leveraging customer identity data securely, businesses can provide relevant and context-aware experiences while ensuring compliance with privacy regulations.

Zero Trust principles should be incorporated into CIAM implementation to enhance security by continuously verifying user identities and device trustworthiness. Unlike traditional perimeter-based security models, Zero Trust assumes that no user or device should be trusted by default. Continuous authentication, session monitoring, and least privilege access policies ensure that users only have access to the resources necessary for their interactions. Organizations should enforce risk-based access control, dynamically adjusting permissions based on user behavior, location, and security posture.

Providing self-service account management capabilities empowers customers to control their authentication preferences, update personal information, and manage consent settings. Self-service options reduce the burden on customer support teams while enhancing user trust and satisfaction. Organizations should offer intuitive user interfaces that allow customers to recover accounts, change authentication methods, and review login activity securely.

Comprehensive logging and monitoring are essential in CIAM implementation to detect security incidents, ensure compliance, and analyze authentication trends. Organizations should integrate CIAM with Security Information and Event Management (SIEM) solutions to monitor login attempts, access patterns, and anomalies. Automated alerts and threat intelligence feeds help security teams respond to suspicious activities in real time, preventing unauthorized access and data breaches.

Ensuring accessibility and inclusivity in CIAM implementation is also critical. Digital identity systems must be designed to accommodate users with disabilities, providing alternative authentication methods such as voice recognition, screen reader compatibility, and adaptable input mechanisms. Organizations should conduct usability testing to identify potential barriers and optimize authentication flows for diverse user needs.

CIAM implementation should be regularly tested and updated to address emerging security threats and evolving business requirements. Organizations should conduct penetration testing, vulnerability assessments, and compliance audits to identify weaknesses and improve security controls. Regular updates to authentication policies, API security, and fraud detection mechanisms ensure that the CIAM system remains resilient against evolving cyber threats.

A successful CIAM implementation requires a balance between security, usability, and compliance. By adopting best practices such as frictionless authentication, adaptive security controls, regulatory compliance, and fraud prevention, businesses can protect customer identities while delivering seamless and personalized digital experiences. Investing in a future-proof CIAM strategy enables organizations to scale securely, build customer trust, and drive engagement across digital ecosystems.

Selecting the Right CIAM Vendor

Choosing the right Customer Identity and Access Management (CIAM) vendor is a critical decision that impacts security, user experience, scalability, and regulatory compliance. Organizations must evaluate CIAM solutions based on their ability to meet business requirements, integrate with existing infrastructure, and provide robust identity management capabilities. A well-selected CIAM vendor enhances authentication processes, protects user data, and enables seamless access across digital platforms while ensuring compliance with industry regulations.

One of the first considerations when selecting a CIAM vendor is security. A strong CIAM solution should include multi-factor authentication (MFA), adaptive authentication, biometric verification, and risk-based authentication to protect against identity fraud and unauthorized access. The vendor should support passwordless authentication methods, such as magic links, one-time passcodes (OTPs), and biometric authentication, to enhance security while reducing friction for users. Additionally, the vendor should implement strong encryption, secure storage of identity data, and protection against credential stuffing and brute-force attacks.

Scalability is another crucial factor in evaluating CIAM vendors. Businesses with large customer bases, e-commerce platforms, financial institutions, and global enterprises require CIAM solutions that can handle millions of authentication requests efficiently. The vendor should provide cloud-native architecture with elastic scalability, ensuring that the system can handle traffic spikes during high-demand periods without performance degradation. Organizations should assess whether the vendor offers regional data centers, load balancing, and auto-scaling capabilities to support global deployments.

Integration with existing business systems is essential for seamless identity management. The CIAM vendor should offer pre-built integrations with popular customer relationship management (CRM) systems, marketing platforms, e-commerce solutions, and enterprise applications. Compatibility with identity standards such as OAuth 2.0, OpenID Connect (OIDC), and Security Assertion Markup Language (SAML) is necessary for ensuring secure authentication across multiple platforms. Organizations should evaluate the vendor's API capabilities, ensuring that developers can customize authentication workflows, manage user identities, and enforce access policies through API-driven integration.

User experience plays a significant role in CIAM selection, as customers expect frictionless authentication and account management. The vendor should provide intuitive user interfaces, social login options, and Single Sign-On (SSO) functionality to simplify access across digital services. Progressive profiling capabilities allow businesses to collect user data gradually, reducing barriers to registration while ensuring compliance with privacy regulations. A CIAM solution that offers self-service account management empowers customers to update personal information, reset passwords, and manage authentication preferences without requiring manual intervention from support teams.

Compliance with regulatory requirements is a key consideration when selecting a CIAM vendor. Data protection laws such as the General Data Protection Regulation (GDPR), California Consumer Privacy Act (CCPA), and industry-specific regulations require businesses to implement strong identity security measures. The vendor should offer built-in consent management, enabling users to control how their data is collected and processed. Role-based access control (RBAC) and attribute-based access control (ABAC) help organizations enforce least-privilege access policies while maintaining compliance with security and privacy standards.

Fraud prevention capabilities are essential for protecting customer identities and preventing account takeovers. A CIAM vendor should incorporate artificial intelligence (AI)-driven fraud detection, behavioral biometrics, and anomaly detection to identify suspicious activities in real time. Features such as device fingerprinting, geolocation-based authentication, and continuous session monitoring enhance security while minimizing the risk of fraudulent transactions. Organizations should assess whether the vendor provides automated threat response mechanisms to block malicious activities and protect customer accounts.

Support for omnichannel authentication is important for businesses that operate across multiple digital touchpoints. The CIAM vendor should enable seamless authentication across web applications, mobile apps, kiosks, IoT devices, and in-person interactions. Cross-channel identity synchronization ensures that customers can access their accounts consistently without redundant login prompts. Vendors offering decentralized identity capabilities, such as blockchain-based identity verification, provide enhanced security and data ownership for customers.

Cost and licensing models vary among CIAM vendors, so organizations should evaluate pricing structures based on their usage requirements. Some vendors charge based on the number of active users, authentication transactions, or feature sets. Businesses should assess whether the vendor offers flexible pricing models that align with their growth plans. Additionally, organizations should consider the total cost of ownership (TCO), including implementation costs, ongoing maintenance, and integration expenses.

Customer support and vendor reliability are critical for ensuring a smooth CIAM deployment and ongoing system management. Organizations should assess the vendor's support offerings, including service level agreements (SLAs), response times, and availability of dedicated support teams. A vendor with a strong track record in identity security, regular security updates, and a commitment to innovation ensures long-term reliability.

Vendor reputation and industry expertise are also important factors in CIAM selection. Businesses should research customer reviews, case studies, and analyst reports to assess vendor credibility. Vendors with experience in serving enterprises across industries such as finance, healthcare, retail, and telecommunications demonstrate the ability to meet diverse identity management needs.

Customization and extensibility options allow businesses to tailor CIAM solutions to their specific requirements. A CIAM vendor should provide flexible identity workflows, customizable authentication policies, and extensible identity attributes. Organizations should evaluate whether the vendor offers low-code or no-code configuration options for modifying user experiences without extensive development effort.

Analytics and reporting capabilities enable organizations to monitor authentication trends, track user behavior, and detect security incidents. A CIAM vendor should offer real-time dashboards, event logging, and compliance reporting to provide insights into identity management activities. AI-powered analytics enhance security by identifying emerging threats, optimizing authentication workflows, and improving fraud prevention strategies.

Mobile-first identity management is essential for businesses with high mobile engagement. A CIAM vendor should support mobile SDKs, in-app authentication, and biometric authentication for mobile devices. Mobile CIAM implementations should provide secure authentication methods such as push notification authentication, mobile OTPs, and adaptive risk assessments.

Zero Trust alignment ensures that CIAM solutions support continuous verification, risk-based access policies, and least-privilege access controls. A vendor that incorporates Zero Trust principles enhances security by enforcing strong authentication at every access request, regardless of user location or network. Organizations should ensure that the CIAM vendor provides real-time identity verification, continuous authentication, and risk-aware access management.

By evaluating CIAM vendors based on security, scalability, integration capabilities, user experience, compliance, fraud prevention, cost, support, reputation, customization, analytics, mobile identity management, and Zero Trust alignment, organizations can select a solution that meets their identity management needs. Investing in a reliable CIAM vendor enhances digital security, improves customer engagement, and enables seamless authentication across digital ecosystems.

Cloud-Based vs. On-Premises CIAM Solutions

Choosing between cloud-based and on-premises Customer Identity and Access Management (CIAM) solutions is a critical decision that affects security, scalability, cost, and operational efficiency. Organizations must evaluate their business needs, regulatory requirements, and infrastructure capabilities to determine the best approach for managing customer identities. While both deployment models offer advantages and challenges, the decision ultimately depends on factors such as control, flexibility, compliance, and long-term maintenance.

Cloud-based CIAM solutions provide businesses with a scalable, managed identity service hosted by a cloud provider. These solutions eliminate the need for organizations to maintain physical infrastructure, reducing the complexity of deployment and ongoing management. Cloud-based CIAM platforms are designed for high availability, ensuring that authentication services remain operational even during traffic spikes, cyber threats, or hardware failures. This makes them ideal for businesses that experience fluctuating user demand, such as e-commerce platforms, financial services, and global enterprises.

One of the primary advantages of cloud-based CIAM is scalability. Cloud solutions automatically adjust resources based on usage, allowing businesses to handle millions of authentication requests efficiently. This elasticity is particularly valuable for organizations with seasonal spikes in user activity, such as retail businesses during holiday sales or streaming platforms during major content releases. The ability to scale on demand ensures a seamless user experience without the need for manual infrastructure adjustments.

Security is a major consideration when evaluating cloud-based CIAM solutions. Leading cloud providers implement robust security measures, including encryption, data redundancy, and real-time threat detection, to protect customer identities. Many cloud CIAM solutions also support Zero Trust security models, enforcing continuous authentication, risk-based access controls, and behavioral analytics to detect suspicious activity. However, organizations must assess the security practices of their cloud provider, ensuring that data encryption, access policies, and compliance controls align with their internal security requirements.

Compliance and data residency requirements influence the decision to adopt cloud-based CIAM. Regulations such as the General Data Protection Regulation (GDPR) and the California Consumer Privacy Act (CCPA) impose strict guidelines on how customer data is stored, processed, and shared. Some cloud CIAM providers offer regional data centers to help businesses comply with data sovereignty laws, but organizations handling highly sensitive data—such as healthcare providers or government agencies—may prefer on-premises solutions to maintain complete control over data storage and access.

Cost efficiency is another key benefit of cloud-based CIAM. Traditional on-premises solutions require significant upfront investment in hardware, software, and maintenance. Cloud CIAM solutions operate on a subscription-based model, allowing businesses to pay for only the resources they use. This reduces capital expenditures while providing predictable operating costs. Cloud vendors also handle infrastructure updates, security patches, and system optimizations, eliminating the burden of manual maintenance for IT teams.

On-premises CIAM solutions provide organizations with full control over their identity management infrastructure. This model is often preferred by businesses with stringent security and compliance requirements, such as financial institutions, defense contractors, and government agencies. On-premises CIAM allows organizations to enforce their own security policies, configure identity workflows to meet specific business needs, and maintain direct oversight of customer data.

Data security is a key advantage of on-premises CIAM, as organizations retain complete ownership of customer identity data. Unlike cloud solutions that rely on third-party providers for data storage and encryption, on-premises deployments allow businesses to implement their own security measures, ensuring that sensitive customer information remains within their controlled environment. This level of control is particularly important for businesses operating in highly regulated industries where data breaches or unauthorized access could lead to severe legal and financial consequences.

Customization and integration flexibility are significant benefits of on-premises CIAM. Organizations can tailor authentication workflows, access control policies, and identity federation mechanisms to align with their specific requirements. Unlike cloud-based solutions, which may have predefined configurations and limited customization options, on-premises CIAM provides deeper integration capabilities with legacy systems, proprietary applications, and enterprise IT environments. Businesses that require complex identity management features, such as custom identity verification processes or advanced access control models, often prefer on-premises solutions for their adaptability.

However, on-premises CIAM comes with operational challenges. Deploying and maintaining an on-premises identity solution requires dedicated IT resources for infrastructure management, software updates, and security patching. Organizations must continuously monitor system performance, implement threat detection measures, and ensure compliance with evolving security standards. The lack of automatic scalability in on-premises deployments means that businesses must plan for capacity increases, requiring additional hardware investments to accommodate growth.

Disaster recovery and business continuity planning are also critical concerns for on-premises CIAM. In cloud-based solutions, redundancy and failover mechanisms ensure high availability, reducing downtime in case of hardware failures or cyberattacks. On-premises deployments require businesses to implement their own disaster recovery strategies, including data backups, failover configurations, and contingency plans to maintain authentication services during unexpected outages. Without a robust disaster recovery plan, on-premises identity systems may face prolonged downtime, impacting customer access and business operations.

Hybrid CIAM solutions offer a middle ground between cloud and on-premises models. A hybrid approach allows businesses to maintain certain identity management functions on-premises while leveraging cloud capabilities for scalability and high availability. This model is particularly beneficial for organizations that require on-premises control over sensitive data while utilizing cloud-based authentication services for public-facing applications. Hybrid CIAM solutions enable businesses to enforce security policies on-premises while taking advantage of cloud-based features such as adaptive authentication, AI-driven fraud detection, and global identity federation.

Organizations must consider their long-term digital strategy when selecting between cloud-based and on-premises CIAM. Businesses undergoing digital transformation, expanding into new markets, or integrating with third-party platforms may benefit from the agility and scalability of cloud-based CIAM. Conversely, organizations prioritizing strict data control, regulatory compliance, and deep system integration may find that on-premises CIAM better aligns with their security and operational goals.

Selecting the right CIAM deployment model requires a thorough evaluation of security requirements, compliance obligations, scalability needs, integration complexity, and total cost of ownership. Cloud-based CIAM offers flexibility, cost efficiency, and rapid deployment, making it ideal for businesses seeking a scalable and managed identity solution. On-premises CIAM provides full data control, enhanced security customization, and compliance assurance, making it the preferred choice for organizations with stringent regulatory requirements. Businesses must assess their identity management needs carefully, ensuring that their CIAM strategy supports both security and user experience while aligning with their long-term business objectives.

CIAM in the Context of Cybersecurity

Customer Identity and Access Management (CIAM) is a fundamental component of modern cybersecurity strategies, providing the necessary mechanisms to authenticate, authorize, and manage user identities while protecting sensitive information from cyber threats. As businesses increasingly operate in digital environments, securing customer identities has become a priority to prevent fraud, data breaches, and unauthorized access. CIAM solutions enhance security by implementing strong authentication methods, enforcing access controls, and continuously monitoring identity-related threats.

One of the primary cybersecurity challenges CIAM addresses is account security. Password-based authentication has long been a weak link in cybersecurity, as users often reuse passwords across multiple sites, making them vulnerable to credential stuffing and phishing attacks. CIAM strengthens authentication by offering passwordless authentication options, such as biometric verification, magic links, and authentication apps. Multi-factor authentication (MFA) further enhances security by requiring additional verification factors, such as OTPs, device-based authentication, or behavioral biometrics, ensuring that even if credentials are compromised, unauthorized access is prevented.

Adaptive authentication is a critical cybersecurity feature in CIAM, allowing organizations to assess risk in real time before granting access. Unlike traditional authentication, which applies static security policies, adaptive authentication evaluates multiple risk signals, including device type, location, IP reputation, and behavioral patterns. If an authentication attempt appears risky—such as an unusual login location or device—CIAM can trigger step-up authentication, requiring additional verification before granting access. This proactive approach minimizes the risk of compromised accounts while maintaining a seamless user experience for legitimate customers.

CIAM plays a significant role in protecting against identity theft and account takeovers, two of the most common cybersecurity threats. Cybercriminals use techniques such as phishing, social engineering, and malware to steal credentials and gain unauthorized access to accounts. AI-powered fraud detection in CIAM analyzes login behaviors, transaction patterns, and anomalies to identify potential account compromise. By continuously monitoring user interactions and flagging suspicious activities, CIAM helps prevent fraudulent transactions and unauthorized access to sensitive customer data.

Data breaches remain a significant cybersecurity concern, and CIAM solutions help mitigate risks by enforcing strict data protection measures. Secure storage of customer credentials is a fundamental requirement, with CIAM platforms implementing hashing, encryption, and tokenization to protect sensitive identity data. Organizations must ensure that customer identities are stored securely and comply with industry regulations such as GDPR, CCPA, and PCI DSS, reducing the risk of regulatory penalties and reputational damage

API security is another critical aspect of CIAM in cybersecurity, as businesses increasingly rely on API-driven integrations to facilitate authentication and identity verification across platforms. CIAM enforces secure API authentication using OAuth 2.0 and OpenID Connect (OIDC), ensuring that only authorized applications can access identity-related services. API security measures such as rate limiting, anomaly detection, and token-based authentication help prevent API abuse, protecting customer identities from credential stuffing attacks and unauthorized data access.

Zero Trust security principles align closely with CIAM, emphasizing continuous verification rather than implicit trust. Traditional security models often assume that users within a network perimeter are trustworthy, but Zero Trust mandates that every access request is authenticated and authorized based on real-time risk assessment. CIAM enables organizations to implement Zero Trust by enforcing continuous authentication, risk-based access controls, and least privilege access policies, ensuring that users only have access to the resources necessary for their interactions.

Compliance with cybersecurity regulations and data privacy laws is a crucial aspect of CIAM. Regulations such as GDPR and CCPA require businesses to protect customer identities, provide transparent consent management, and allow users to control their personal information. CIAM solutions integrate consent management features that enable users to review, modify, or revoke consent for data processing. Automated compliance reporting and audit logging further help organizations demonstrate regulatory adherence while ensuring that customer identity data is managed securely.

The rise of artificial intelligence (AI) and machine learning (ML) has significantly enhanced the cybersecurity capabilities of CIAM. AI-driven identity analytics detect patterns of abnormal behavior that may indicate fraudulent activity, allowing organizations to respond proactively to security threats. ML algorithms continuously improve fraud detection models by analyzing authentication attempts, login success rates, and device interactions, enabling CIAM to adapt to emerging cyber threats.

Secure session management is another critical cybersecurity function of CIAM, ensuring that authenticated sessions remain protected from hijacking attempts. CIAM solutions enforce session timeout policies, prevent simultaneous logins from multiple devices, and detect unusual session behaviors that may indicate account compromise. Continuous session monitoring enables organizations to detect unauthorized session takeovers and respond with automated security actions, such as session termination or forced reauthentication.

Behavioral biometrics enhance CIAM cybersecurity by providing an additional layer of identity verification. Unlike traditional

146

authentication, which relies on static credentials, behavioral biometrics analyze how users interact with devices and applications. Factors such as typing speed, mouse movements, touchscreen gestures, and navigation patterns create a unique behavioral profile for each user. CIAM solutions leveraging behavioral biometrics can detect and block fraudulent activities without disrupting legitimate user experiences.

Decentralized identity and blockchain technology are emerging trends in CIAM cybersecurity, offering new ways to manage and verify identities securely. Decentralized identity shifts control from centralized identity providers to individuals, allowing users to store and manage their credentials in secure digital wallets. Blockchain-based identity verification ensures that identity attributes remain tamper-proof and verifiable across multiple platforms, reducing the risk of identity fraud and data breaches.

CIAM also plays a vital role in securing Internet of Things (IoT) environments, where connected devices must authenticate securely to prevent unauthorized access. IoT CIAM solutions assign unique identities to devices, enabling secure authentication and access control. Device identity management prevents unauthorized devices from interacting with sensitive networks, mitigating cybersecurity risks in smart home, industrial, and healthcare IoT applications.

Threat intelligence integration strengthens CIAM cybersecurity by enabling real-time detection of compromised credentials and security threats. CIAM platforms integrate with global threat intelligence feeds to identify credentials leaked in data breaches, block known malicious IP addresses, and enforce security policies dynamically based on emerging threats. Automated threat response mechanisms help organizations mitigate risks proactively, preventing identity-related security incidents before they escalate.

By aligning with cybersecurity best practices, CIAM ensures that organizations can manage customer identities securely while protecting against fraud, identity theft, and unauthorized access. The integration of adaptive authentication, AI-driven fraud detection, Zero Trust principles, and secure API authentication makes CIAM a critical component of modern cybersecurity strategies. Organizations that implement CIAM effectively enhance digital trust, ensure regulatory compliance, and safeguard customer identities in an increasingly connected digital world.

The Cost of Poor CIAM Implementation

A poorly implemented Customer Identity and Access Management (CIAM) solution can have severe consequences for businesses, affecting security, user experience, regulatory compliance, and overall operational efficiency. In a digital-first world where customer identity is at the center of online interactions, organizations that fail to deploy a robust CIAM strategy risk financial losses, reputational damage, and loss of customer trust. The costs of inadequate CIAM implementation extend beyond technical challenges, impacting revenue, regulatory standing, and competitive positioning in the market.

One of the most immediate and severe consequences of poor CIAM implementation is security vulnerability. Weak authentication mechanisms, improperly configured access controls, and outdated security protocols expose businesses to cyber threats such as account takeovers, credential stuffing, and identity fraud. If an organization does not implement multi-factor authentication (MFA), adaptive authentication, or risk-based authentication, attackers can exploit weak credentials to gain unauthorized access to user accounts. This can lead to fraudulent transactions, data theft, and compliance violations, all of which carry significant financial and legal implications.

Data breaches are among the most expensive outcomes of a poorly managed CIAM system. If customer identity data is not adequately protected through encryption, hashing, or secure storage practices, attackers can exfiltrate sensitive information, including usernames, passwords, payment details, and personally identifiable information (PII). The financial impact of a data breach includes regulatory fines, legal fees, compensation for affected customers, and the cost of incident response efforts. In addition to financial losses, businesses also suffer reputational damage that can lead to customer churn and loss of market confidence.

Regulatory non-compliance is another costly consequence of inadequate CIAM implementation. Data protection laws such as the General Data Protection Regulation (GDPR), the California Consumer Privacy Act (CCPA), and industry-specific regulations impose strict requirements on how customer identities and personal data should be managed. Organizations that fail to implement proper CIAM controls, including user consent management, data encryption, and access logs, face substantial fines and legal repercussions. In some cases, businesses may be forced to suspend operations or undergo extensive compliance audits, resulting in additional costs and disruptions.

Poor CIAM implementation can also lead to a degraded user experience, directly affecting customer engagement and retention. If authentication flows are overly complex, requiring unnecessary steps or frequent reauthentication, customers may abandon registration processes or opt for competitors that offer smoother experiences. Friction in authentication, such as slow login times, cumbersome password reset processes, or lack of Single Sign-On (SSO), contributes to frustration and reduced conversion rates. Businesses that fail to prioritize seamless and secure user authentication risk losing customers to competitors with more efficient identity management solutions.

Account recovery issues are another symptom of poor CIAM design. If users experience difficulties recovering lost passwords or unlocking suspended accounts, they may resort to creating multiple accounts, leading to duplicate customer records and inaccurate user data. A poorly structured CIAM system without self-service account recovery options increases the burden on customer support teams, leading to higher operational costs and inefficiencies. Organizations must invest in intuitive self-service options, including passwordless authentication and secure account recovery mechanisms, to reduce support inquiries and improve customer satisfaction.

Scalability issues arise when CIAM solutions are not designed to handle high volumes of authentication requests. Businesses with growing customer bases or seasonal spikes in traffic—such as e-commerce platforms during holiday sales—require CIAM systems that can scale dynamically. A poorly implemented CIAM solution may struggle with increased demand, resulting in slow authentication times, login failures, and system downtime. These disruptions negatively impact revenue generation, especially for businesses that rely on digital transactions and continuous user engagement.

Fraud and identity theft risks increase significantly when CIAM is not properly configured to detect and prevent fraudulent activities. Attackers exploit weak identity verification processes to create fake accounts, commit payment fraud, and manipulate loyalty programs. Without AI-driven fraud detection, behavioral analytics, or risk-based authentication, businesses face substantial financial losses from fraudulent transactions and chargebacks. Fraudulent activities not only lead to direct financial losses but also erode trust among legitimate customers, damaging brand reputation.

API security weaknesses further compound the risks of poor CIAM implementation. Many businesses integrate third-party services, mobile applications, and partner platforms using APIs, making secure API authentication a critical component of CIAM. If CIAM does not enforce OAuth 2.0, OpenID Connect (OIDC), or secure token-based authentication, attackers can exploit API vulnerabilities to gain unauthorized access to customer identity data. API breaches can result in data leaks, unauthorized transactions, and loss of intellectual property, all of which contribute to financial and reputational damage.

Lack of integration with existing business systems also leads to inefficiencies and missed opportunities. CIAM should seamlessly integrate with customer relationship management (CRM) platforms, marketing automation tools, and e-commerce systems to enable personalized user experiences and data-driven decision-making. If CIAM operates in isolation, businesses may struggle with fragmented customer identities, inconsistent user profiles, and redundant authentication processes across different platforms. This leads to operational inefficiencies and lost revenue opportunities from poorly targeted marketing campaigns or disconnected customer experiences.

Businesses that fail to implement effective CIAM strategies also risk falling behind in innovation and digital transformation. Modern CIAM solutions support decentralized identity, blockchain-based authentication, and AI-driven security enhancements. Organizations that rely on outdated or legacy CIAM systems miss out on opportunities to enhance security, reduce fraud, and improve user experience through emerging technologies. Failing to modernize CIAM infrastructure limits an organization's ability to compete in a digital economy where secure, seamless, and personalized identity management is a differentiating factor.

To mitigate the costs of poor CIAM implementation, organizations must prioritize identity security, user experience, compliance, and scalability from the outset. Investing in a robust CIAM solution ensures that authentication processes are secure, efficient, and user-friendly, while reducing exposure to cyber threats, fraud, and regulatory penalties. A well-implemented CIAM strategy not only enhances security but also drives customer engagement, operational efficiency, and business growth in an increasingly digital landscape.

The Role of CIAM in Customer Retention

Customer Identity and Access Management (CIAM) plays a crucial role in customer retention by ensuring seamless, secure, and personalized digital experiences. Businesses today operate in a highly competitive environment where customer expectations for convenience, security, and personalization continue to rise. A well-implemented CIAM solution helps organizations maintain customer trust, reduce friction in authentication, and provide consistent experiences across multiple touchpoints, all of which contribute to long-term customer loyalty.

One of the most significant factors influencing customer retention is ease of access. A cumbersome or complicated authentication process can frustrate users, leading to account abandonment and decreased engagement. CIAM solutions streamline authentication through features such as Single Sign-On (SSO), passwordless authentication, and social login. SSO allows customers to log in once and gain access to multiple services without needing to re-enter credentials repeatedly. Passwordless authentication, including biometric authentication and one-time passcodes (OTPs), eliminates the friction associated with remembering and resetting passwords. Social login enables users to authenticate using existing credentials from providers such as Google, Facebook, or Apple, reducing registration and login barriers.

Security is a critical component of customer retention. Customers expect their personal and financial data to be protected at all times. A CIAM solution that integrates multi-factor authentication (MFA), adaptive authentication, and risk-based access control ensures that security measures are in place without adding unnecessary complexity. Adaptive authentication dynamically adjusts security requirements based on contextual factors such as device, location, and login behavior. If an authentication attempt is deemed low-risk, the system allows seamless access. However, if the system detects anomalies—such as an unfamiliar location or unusual transaction patterns—it prompts additional verification steps to protect customer accounts.

Trust plays a vital role in customer loyalty, and CIAM strengthens this trust by ensuring transparency and control over personal data. Data protection regulations such as the General Data Protection Regulation (GDPR) and the California Consumer Privacy Act (CCPA) require businesses to provide users with clear consent management and privacy controls. A well-implemented CIAM solution includes built-in consent management, allowing customers to manage their data preferences, opt in or out of marketing communications, and control how their personal information is shared. When businesses demonstrate a commitment to privacy and security, customers are more likely to continue engaging with their services.

Personalization is another key factor in customer retention, and CIAM enables businesses to deliver tailored experiences based on user preferences and behavior. By collecting and securely managing customer identity data, CIAM allows businesses to offer personalized recommendations, targeted promotions, and customized content. Progressive profiling enables organizations to collect customer data gradually, improving personalization without overwhelming users with lengthy registration forms. When customers receive relevant and timely content based on their interests and past interactions, they are more likely to remain loyal to the brand.

Omnichannel consistency is essential for maintaining customer engagement across various digital platforms. Customers expect a seamless experience whether they are accessing a website, mobile app, or in-store kiosk. CIAM ensures that customer identities remain synchronized across all channels, enabling a unified experience regardless of the device or platform used. If a customer starts a shopping session on a mobile app and later switches to a desktop website, CIAM ensures that their authentication status, shopping cart, and preferences remain intact. This level of consistency enhances user satisfaction and encourages continued engagement.

Customer self-service capabilities contribute to retention by empowering users to manage their accounts independently. A robust CIAM solution provides self-service account management features, allowing customers to reset passwords, update contact information, manage authentication preferences, and review login activity without requiring assistance from customer support. This reduces frustration and increases customer satisfaction, as users can resolve common account-related issues quickly and securely.

Fraud prevention is another critical aspect of customer retention. If a customer's account is compromised due to weak identity management practices, trust in the organization is severely damaged, leading to potential churn. CIAM integrates AI-driven fraud detection, behavioral biometrics, and anomaly detection to identify and prevent fraudulent activities before they impact customers. By continuously monitoring user behavior and detecting suspicious login attempts, CIAM protects customers from identity theft and account takeovers, reinforcing confidence in the platform.

Loyalty programs are a powerful tool for customer retention, and CIAM enhances their effectiveness by ensuring secure and seamless access. Customers should be able to log in easily to view and redeem rewards, track points, and receive personalized offers without encountering authentication hurdles. CIAM solutions integrate with loyalty program platforms to provide a frictionless experience, ensuring that customers remain engaged and incentivized to continue interacting with the brand.

Customer retention also depends on businesses being able to analyze and respond to user behavior effectively. CIAM provides valuable insights into authentication trends, user engagement patterns, and security risks. Organizations can leverage these insights to optimize authentication workflows, identify at-risk customers, and implement proactive engagement strategies. For example, if a customer has not logged in for an extended period, businesses can trigger personalized re-engagement campaigns, such as offering exclusive discounts or reminding them of saved items in their cart.

The role of CIAM in customer retention extends beyond security and authentication—it encompasses trust, convenience, personalization, and engagement. A seamless and secure identity management experience encourages customers to continue using a platform, reducing churn and increasing lifetime value. By prioritizing ease of access, data security, personalized interactions, and omnichannel consistency, businesses can create an identity experience that fosters long-term customer loyalty.

Case Studies: Successful CIAM Implementations

Customer Identity and Access Management (CIAM) has transformed how businesses manage user authentication, data security, and customer experiences. Organizations across various industries have successfully implemented CIAM to enhance security, improve customer engagement, and comply with regulatory requirements. By examining real-world case studies, it becomes clear how CIAM solutions address challenges such as fraud prevention, frictionless authentication, and scalability while delivering tangible business benefits.

One of the most notable CIAM success stories comes from a global e-commerce company that struggled with high cart abandonment rates due to cumbersome authentication processes. The company required customers to create accounts and set up passwords before making purchases, which led to significant user drop-offs. By implementing a CIAM solution with social login, passwordless authentication, and Single Sign-On (SSO), the company drastically reduced authentication friction. Customers could log in using their existing social media credentials or receive magic links via email, allowing them to complete purchases without remembering complex passwords. As a result, the company saw a 25% increase in conversion rates and a 40% reduction in password-related customer support requests.

A major financial institution successfully leveraged CIAM to strengthen fraud prevention and regulatory compliance. With increasing incidents of account takeovers and identity fraud, the bank needed a more secure yet user-friendly authentication method. The institution implemented a CIAM platform with adaptive authentication, biometric login, and AI-driven fraud detection. The new system analyzed real-time risk signals such as device reputation, geolocation, and transaction patterns to determine authentication requirements dynamically. If a login attempt appeared suspicious, step-up authentication was triggered, requiring additional verification. This approach reduced fraudulent account access by 60% while ensuring compliance with stringent financial regulations, including PSD2 and GDPR.

A global streaming service faced challenges in managing millions of customer identities across multiple platforms, including smart TVs, mobile apps, and web browsers. The company needed a CIAM solution that could provide seamless authentication while maintaining strong security controls. By integrating a cloud based CIAM solution with federated identity management and API security, the streaming service enabled users to log in once and access content across all devices without repeated authentication prompts. The solution also included rate-limiting mechanisms to prevent credential stuffing attacks and unauthorized API requests. As a result, user retention improved, and customer complaints about login difficulties decreased by 50%.

The healthcare industry has also benefited from CIAM implementations, particularly in telemedicine and patient portal security. A leading telehealth provider struggled with patient authentication issues, as many users forgot their login credentials or faced security concerns when accessing medical records. By implementing passwordless authentication and biometric verification, the company improved patient access while ensuring HIPAA compliance. Patients could use fingerprint or facial recognition on mobile devices to securely log in to their accounts without passwords. The implementation led to a 70% reduction in password reset requests and an overall increase in telehealth session participation, as users found the authentication process more convenient and secure.

A multinational retail chain implemented CIAM to unify customer identities across online and in-store experiences. Previously, customers had to create separate accounts for e-commerce transactions and loyalty program participation. This fragmented approach led to inconsistent user experiences and difficulties in tracking customer preferences. The retailer adopted a CIAM solution that provided a unified identity for customers, enabling them to use the same login credentials for online shopping, in-store kiosks, and mobile loyalty apps. The system also included progressive profiling, allowing customers to provide additional information over time instead of requiring lengthy registration forms. This led to a 30% increase in loyalty program sign-ups and a higher level of personalized customer engagement.

A global travel and hospitality company faced challenges in providing secure and seamless login experiences for customers booking flights, hotels, and rental services. The company's existing authentication system was outdated and caused frequent login failures, leading to poor customer satisfaction. The implementation of a modern CIAM solution introduced SSO, adaptive authentication, and self-service account management. Travelers could now log in once and access all travel services without repeated authentication steps. The system also provided dynamic authentication based on travel risk factors, such as location and transaction amount. By improving authentication efficiency, the company reduced login failures by 45% and increased repeat bookings by 20%.

A leading telecommunications provider needed a CIAM solution to enhance customer identity security while improving user experiences across its digital services. Customers often faced difficulties managing multiple accounts for mobile plans, internet services, and streaming subscriptions. The company deployed a centralized CIAM system that consolidated all digital services under a single identity. This allowed customers to manage their accounts more easily while enabling strong security measures such as MFA and behavioral biometrics. By reducing authentication complexity and improving security, the company saw a 35% increase in customer satisfaction scores and a decline in fraudulent account activity.

A major government agency dealing with digital citizen services successfully implemented CIAM to streamline authentication for various online portals. Citizens previously had to register separately for tax filing, healthcare benefits, and public records access. The agency introduced a federated identity management system that enabled users to authenticate once and gain secure access to multiple government services. The CIAM solution also included consent management, ensuring that users had full control over their personal data. This transformation resulted in a 50% decrease in login-related service inquiries and increased citizen engagement with digital government services.

A top-tier university faced identity management challenges with student and faculty access to online learning platforms, campus resources, and research portals. The institution implemented a CIAM solution with role-based access control (RBAC), ensuring that students, faculty, and administrative staff had appropriate permissions based on their roles. The system also provided seamless integration with third-party educational platforms, allowing students to access coursework and research materials without authentication disruptions. As a result, login success rates improved, and the institution reported a 40% decrease in IT support tickets related to account access issues.

Successful CIAM implementations across industries demonstrate the importance of secure, user-friendly authentication and identity management. Organizations that adopt CIAM effectively not only enhance security and compliance but also improve customer satisfaction, streamline access to services, and drive business growth. By prioritizing seamless authentication, fraud prevention, and scalable identity solutions, businesses can optimize their digital experiences and foster long-term customer relationships.

Common Pitfalls and How to Avoid Them

Implementing Customer Identity and Access Management (CIAM) is a complex process that requires careful planning, security considerations, and a user-centric approach. Many organizations encounter pitfalls that undermine the effectiveness of their CIAM strategy, leading to security vulnerabilities, poor user experiences, and compliance risks. Understanding these common mistakes and adopting best practices helps businesses build a robust and scalable identity management system that balances security with usability.

One of the most frequent pitfalls in CIAM implementation is prioritizing security over user experience without finding a balance. While strong authentication measures are essential, an overly rigid authentication process can frustrate users, leading to abandoned registrations, higher churn rates, and increased customer support requests. Organizations that force complex password policies, frequent re-authentication, or mandatory multi-factor authentication (MFA) for every login create unnecessary friction. To avoid this issue, businesses should implement adaptive authentication, which dynamically adjusts security requirements based on user risk levels. Low-risk users should experience minimal authentication friction, while high-risk actions, such as accessing sensitive data from a new device, should trigger additional verification steps.

Another common mistake is failing to provide a seamless omnichannel experience. Customers interact with businesses across multiple devices and platforms, including websites, mobile apps, in-store kiosks, and call centers. If authentication mechanisms are inconsistent across these touchpoints, users may encounter repeated login prompts, session expirations, or difficulties accessing their accounts. CIAM solutions must support Single Sign-On (SSO) and federated identity management to ensure a seamless authentication experience across all digital channels. Businesses should also integrate progressive profiling to collect customer information gradually instead of requiring lengthy registration forms, improving conversion rates while maintaining data integrity.

Weak password policies and reliance on outdated authentication methods expose organizations to security threats such as credential stuffing and phishing attacks. Many businesses still allow customers to use weak passwords, fail to enforce password rotation policies, or rely solely on email-based authentication, which can be exploited through social engineering. A well-implemented CIAM strategy should include strong passwordless authentication options, such as biometrics, passkeys, or time-sensitive authentication links. Implementing MFA should be encouraged, but it should also be user-friendly, incorporating options like push notifications or authentication apps instead of SMS-based OTPs, which are susceptible to SIM-swapping attacks.

Failure to protect APIs is another critical oversight in CIAM deployments. Many organizations integrate third-party services, mobile applications, and partner platforms using APIs, but they often neglect to implement proper API security measures. If CIAM-related APIs are not secured using OAuth 2.0, OpenID Connect (OIDC), or token-based authentication, attackers can exploit these vulnerabilities to gain unauthorized access to customer data. To mitigate this risk, businesses should enforce strict API authentication and authorization policies, implement rate limiting to prevent automated attacks, and continuously monitor API activity for anomalies.

Lack of compliance with data privacy regulations is a major pitfall that can lead to legal penalties and reputational damage. Regulations such as the General Data Protection Regulation (GDPR) and the California Consumer Privacy Act (CCPA) impose strict requirements on how customer Identity data is collected, stored, and processed. Many businesses overlook consent management, fail to provide users with clear data privacy controls, or lack proper audit logging for compliance tracking. CIAM solutions should integrate consent management portals, allowing users to review and modify their data-sharing preferences easily. Organizations must also implement transparent data retention policies, ensuring that customer identities are stored only for the necessary duration.

Scalability challenges arise when businesses deploy a CIAM system that cannot handle increased authentication requests during peak periods. E-commerce platforms, financial services, and streaming services often experience traffic spikes during sales events, product launches, or major content releases. If CIAM infrastructure is not designed for scalability, users may experience login failures, session timeouts, and degraded performance. Organizations should opt for cloud-based CIAM solutions with elastic scalability, ensuring that authentication services can dynamically scale based on demand. Load balancing and distributed authentication nodes further enhance system reliability, preventing outages during high-traffic events.

Poor customer support and lack of self-service options create frustration for users who need to manage their authentication settings, recover accounts, or reset passwords. If customers are forced to contact support teams for simple account recovery tasks, it increases operational costs while degrading the user experience. A well-implemented CIAM system should include self-service portals that allow users to reset passwords, update authentication preferences, and review login activity independently. Organizations should also provide clear security notifications and alerts, informing customers of account changes and potential security risks.

Neglecting fraud detection mechanisms is another major pitfall in CIAM implementation. Cybercriminals use techniques such as bot-driven credential stuffing, account takeovers, and fake account creation to exploit weak identity management systems. If CIAM lacks AI-driven fraud detection, businesses may struggle to identify and mitigate fraudulent activities in real time. Organizations should integrate behavioral analytics, device fingerprinting, and machine learning algorithms to detect suspicious authentication patterns. Risk-based authentication should be enforced for high-value transactions or unusual login attempts, ensuring that fraud is blocked before it impacts users.

Failure to future-proof CIAM investments leads to technical debt and system inefficiencies. Many businesses implement CIAM solutions without considering long-term scalability, technology evolution, or integration capabilities. Legacy identity systems often lack support for emerging authentication technologies, such as decentralized identity, blockchain-based authentication, or biometric advancements. Organizations should select CIAM solutions that support open standards, modular integrations, and continuous security updates to ensure long-term viability.

Data silos caused by disconnected CIAM systems hinder a business's ability to create personalized user experiences. If identity data is fragmented across multiple systems—such as separate authentication databases for web, mobile, and in-store services—organizations struggle to deliver a unified customer experience. A centralized CIAM platform with identity federation capabilities ensures that customer identities remain synchronized across all digital properties. Businesses should prioritize data unification, enabling seamless access while maintaining strong security controls.

By addressing these common pitfalls, organizations can deploy CIAM solutions that enhance security, improve user experience, and ensure regulatory compliance. A proactive approach to identity management ensures that authentication processes remain seamless, fraud risks are minimized, and customer engagement is strengthened. Businesses that prioritize well-structured CIAM implementations gain a competitive edge by fostering trust, reducing friction, and creating secure digital interactions that keep customers coming back.

Measuring CIAM Success: KPIs and Metrics

Implementing a Customer Identity and Access Management (CIAM) solution is only the first step toward enhancing security, user experience, and regulatory compliance. To ensure that CIAM delivers the intended benefits, organizations must continuously measure its effectiveness using key performance indicators (KPIs) and metrics. These metrics provide insights into authentication efficiency, security posture, user engagement, and system performance, allowing businesses to optimize their CIAM strategy and improve customer satisfaction.

One of the most critical KPIs for measuring CIAM success is authentication success rate. This metric tracks the percentage of successful login attempts compared to total authentication requests. A high success rate indicates that users can access their accounts without unnecessary friction, while a low success rate suggests authentication failures due to incorrect credentials, system errors, or ineffective authentication methods. Businesses should monitor authentication success rates across different channels—web, mobile, and APIs—to identify potential issues affecting specific platforms.

Closely related to authentication success is the password reset rate, which measures how frequently users request password resets. A high password reset rate often indicates that users are struggling with password-based authentication, leading to frustration and increased support costs. Organizations aiming to reduce password reset rates should consider implementing passwordless authentication, Single Sign-On (SSO), and biometric login options. Monitoring password reset trends over time helps organizations assess the impact of alternative authentication methods on user convenience.

Multi-Factor Authentication (MFA) adoption rate is another essential CIAM metric, tracking how many users enable MFA for their accounts. MFA significantly enhances security by requiring additional authentication factors beyond a password. However, if MFA adoption rates remain low, businesses must evaluate whether the enrollment process is too complex or if users perceive MFA as inconvenient. Encouraging MFA adoption through user education, incentives, or adaptive authentication can improve security without introducing excessive friction.

The average authentication time measures how long it takes for users to complete the login process. Long authentication times can frustrate customers and lead to higher abandonment rates, especially in industries where quick access is critical, such as e-commerce and financial services. Businesses should strive for a balance between security and efficiency by optimizing authentication workflows, reducing unnecessary steps, and implementing adaptive authentication to streamline the process for low-risk users.

The customer onboarding completion rate is a crucial metric for assessing how effectively new users register and verify their identities. A low onboarding completion rate suggests friction in the registration process, such as requiring too much information upfront, slow identity verification, or confusing user interfaces. Implementing progressive profiling, social login, and automated identity verification can improve completion rates and ensure that users complete the registration process without unnecessary obstacles.

Single Sign-On (SSO) adoption rate tracks how many users take advantage of SSO to access multiple services with a single authentication. SSO enhances user convenience by reducing the need for multiple login credentials, but low adoption rates may indicate that users are unaware of the feature or that it is not properly integrated across digital properties. Businesses should analyze SSO usage patterns and ensure seamless integration across all customer-facing platforms to maximize adoption.

Session abandonment rate measures the percentage of users who abandon a session after starting an authentication process but failing to complete it. High abandonment rates indicate usability issues, such as complex login flows, slow authentication response times, or a lack of alternative login options. Reducing session abandonment requires optimizing the login experience, providing passwordless authentication options, and ensuring that authentication flows are intuitive and mobile-friendly.

The fraud detection rate evaluates the effectiveness of CIAM security measures in identifying and blocking fraudulent activities. This metric includes the number of blocked account takeover attempts, detected credential stuffing attacks, and fraudulent login attempts. A high fraud detection rate indicates that the CIAM solution is effectively preventing security threats, but businesses must also ensure that legitimate users are not being falsely flagged as fraudulent, which can lead to poor user experiences.

Customer support inquiries related to authentication provide insights into how well the CIAM system is performing from a usability perspective. A high volume of authentication-related support requests suggests that users are experiencing difficulties with login processes, password resets, or account recovery. Analyzing common support issues helps businesses identify pain points and implement self-service solutions, such as intuitive account recovery options and AI-powered virtual assistants.

Consent management engagement measures how often users review, modify, or revoke their data-sharing preferences. Compliance with privacy regulations such as GDPR and CCPA requires businesses to provide clear and transparent consent management options. If users rarely engage with consent management settings, organizations should improve visibility, user education, and accessibility of privacy controls to build trust and maintain regulatory compliance.

API authentication success rate is a critical metric for businesses that rely on API-driven integrations. It tracks the percentage of successful API authentication attempts compared to total requests. A low success rate may indicate misconfigured API security settings, token expiration issues, or unauthorized access attempts. Businesses should ensure that API authentication follows best practices, including OAuth 2.0, OpenID Connect (OIDC), and token-based access control.

The latency of authentication services measures the time it takes for authentication requests to be processed. High latency can lead to slow logins, degraded user experiences, and increased frustration. CIAM solutions must be optimized for performance, with load balancing, caching mechanisms, and cloud scalability ensuring fast authentication responses even during peak traffic periods.

Retention rate of authenticated users tracks how often users return to the platform after authenticating. A high retention rate suggests that users find value in the digital service and trust the authentication system. Low retention rates may indicate that users face authentication challenges, lack engagement, or have concerns about security. Businesses should analyze authentication retention trends and implement improvements to enhance user satisfaction.

Conversion rate of registered users to active users assesses how many users who create accounts actively use the platform over time. High conversion rates indicate that the CIAM system effectively supports user engagement, while low rates suggest that friction in authentication or access control may be discouraging users from returning.

Regularly measuring these CIAM KPIs and metrics enables businesses to make data-driven decisions, optimize authentication workflows, and enhance security while maintaining a seamless customer experience. Organizations should continuously refine their CIAM strategies, ensuring that their identity management solutions remain efficient, scalable, and aligned with evolving customer expectations.

The Future of CIAM: Trends and Predictions

Customer Identity and Access Management (CIAM) continues to evolve as businesses prioritize security, seamless user experiences, and regulatory compliance in an increasingly digital world. As cyber threats become more sophisticated and consumer expectations for frictionless authentication grow, CIAM solutions must adapt to meet these challenges. Emerging technologies such as decentralized identity, artificial intelligence (AI)-driven authentication, and passwordless login are shaping the future of CIAM, transforming how organizations manage customer identities while enhancing security and convenience.

One of the most significant trends in CIAM is the shift toward passwordless authentication. Traditional passwords have long been a weak point in identity security, leading to credential stuffing attacks, phishing scams, and account takeovers. Businesses are increasingly adopting passwordless authentication methods such as biometric authentication, FIDO2-based passkeys, and magic links to eliminate the reliance on passwords. By leveraging fingerprint scans, facial recognition, or hardware security keys, organizations reduce friction while improving security. As more companies integrate passwordless authentication into their CIAM strategies, users will experience faster, more secure access to digital services without the risks associated with password management.

Decentralized identity is another emerging trend that is expected to reshape CIAM in the coming years. Traditional identity management models rely on centralized databases where user credentials and personal information are stored. However, these centralized systems are attractive targets for cybercriminals, leading to massive data breaches. Decentralized identity, powered by blockchain technology and self-sovereign identity (SSI) principles, shifts control of identity data from organizations to individuals. Users can store their identity credentials in digital wallets and share only the necessary information with service providers. This approach enhances privacy, reduces data breaches, and allows users to have greater control over their personal information. Governments and enterprises are already exploring decentralized identity frameworks for secure identity verification, and adoption is expected to grow as regulatory support increases.

The integration of artificial intelligence and machine learning into CIAM solutions is revolutionizing how authentication and fraud detection are managed. AI-driven behavioral biometrics analyze user interactions, such as typing patterns, mouse movements, and mobile gestures, to create a unique behavioral profile for each user. If an authentication attempt deviates from the usual behavior, the system can trigger additional verification or block access altogether. Machine learning models continuously improve fraud detection capabilities by identifying new attack patterns, reducing false positives, and adapting to evolving security threats. As AI technology matures, CIAM solutions will become more intelligent, automating identity verification processes while minimizing friction for legitimate users.

Adaptive authentication and risk-based access control are becoming essential components of modern CIAM strategies. Instead of applying static authentication rules to all users, adaptive authentication evaluates risk factors such as device reputation, login location, and transaction history to determine the appropriate level of security. For example, a user logging in from a trusted device in a familiar location may be granted immediate access, while a login attempt from an unusual IP address may trigger multi-factor authentication. This dynamic approach enhances security while maintaining a seamless user experience. As more businesses adopt Zero Trust security models, adaptive authentication will play a crucial role in ensuring continuous identity verification.

Regulatory compliance will continue to drive CIAM innovation, as businesses must adhere to evolving data protection laws and privacy regulations. Stricter identity verification requirements are expected, particularly in financial services, healthcare, and government sectors.

Regulations such as the General Data Protection Regulation (GDPR), California Consumer Privacy Act (CCPA), and the upcoming European Digital Identity Framework will require organizations to enhance data security, enforce strong authentication measures, and provide transparent consent management options. CIAM solutions will need to incorporate advanced privacy controls, automated compliance reporting, and consent management tools to help businesses meet these regulatory requirements efficiently.

Omnichannel identity management is another key trend shaping the future of CIAM. Customers expect a consistent authentication experience across all digital and physical touchpoints, including web applications, mobile apps, IoT devices, and in-person interactions. CIAM solutions must provide unified identity management that allows users to authenticate once and seamlessly access services across multiple platforms. Businesses are increasingly integrating CIAM with customer relationship management (CRM) systems, marketing platforms, and loyalty programs to deliver personalized experiences based on customer identity data. As omnichannel strategies expand, CIAM platforms will need to support identity federation, cross-device authentication, and real-time identity synchronization.

The growth of IoT and connected devices presents new challenges and opportunities for CIAM. As more devices connect to digital ecosystems, securing device identities becomes as important as securing human identities. CIAM solutions will need to incorporate device authentication mechanisms, ensuring that only authorized devices can access sensitive data and services. The use of AI-driven device fingerprinting, cryptographic authentication, and decentralized identity frameworks will become more prevalent in securing IoT environments. Businesses adopting IoT-based solutions must ensure that their CIAM strategies extend beyond traditional user authentication to include device identity governance.

Biometric authentication advancements will continue to shape the future of CIAM, moving beyond traditional fingerprint and facial recognition. Emerging biometric technologies, such as voice recognition, iris scanning, and even heartbeat authentication, are being explored to provide more secure and user-friendly authentication options. Continuous authentication, where identity verification occurs in the background without explicit user interaction, is expected to become more widespread. This approach enhances security without disrupting the user experience, ensuring that identity verification happens seamlessly throughout the session.

Another evolving trend in CIAM is the convergence of identity and cybersecurity. As cyber threats become more sophisticated, CIAM will play an even greater role in securing user identities and preventing fraud. Identity Threat Detection and Response (ITDR) is an emerging security approach that focuses on detecting and mitigating identity-based threats in real time. Organizations are integrating CIAM with Security Information and Event Management (SIEM) and Extended Detection and Response (XDR) platforms to enhance threat intelligence and automated response capabilities. The fusion of identity management and cybersecurity will become a standard practice, ensuring that CIAM not only facilitates authentication but also actively protects against cyberattacks.

The rise of context-aware authentication is another trend that will influence CIAM in the coming years. Context-aware authentication goes beyond traditional authentication factors by analyzing real-time environmental data, such as the user's location, device usage patterns, and network security posture. This approach allows CIAM systems to dynamically adjust authentication requirements based on real-world conditions. If a login attempt occurs from a secure corporate network, minimal authentication may be required, but if the same attempt happens from an untrusted network, additional security measures will be enforced.

As digital ecosystems continue to expand, businesses will need to invest in CIAM solutions that are scalable, secure, and adaptable to emerging threats and technological advancements. The evolution of CIAM will be driven by the need for enhanced user experiences, robust security, and compliance with global regulations. Organizations that embrace these trends will be better positioned to protect customer identities, streamline authentication processes, and deliver seamless, secure digital interactions across all platforms.

How CIAM Supports Digital Identity Ecosystems

Customer Identity and Access Management (CIAM) plays a critical role in the broader digital identity ecosystem, providing businesses with the tools to securely authenticate users, manage access, and protect personal information. As organizations expand their digital presence, they must ensure that customers can interact seamlessly across various platforms while maintaining privacy and security. CIAM solutions facilitate interoperability within digital identity ecosystems by enabling secure authentication, identity federation, and compliance with global data protection regulations.

A digital identity ecosystem consists of multiple entities, including identity providers, relying parties, users, and regulatory bodies, all interacting to facilitate secure and verified access to online services. CIAM serves as the backbone of this ecosystem, ensuring that identity credentials are issued, stored, and shared securely. By implementing standards-based authentication mechanisms such as OAuth 2.0, OpenID Connect (OIDC), and Security Assertion Markup Language (SAML), CIAM solutions enable seamless identity verification across multiple service providers without requiring users to create separate accounts for each platform.

One of the most significant ways CIAM supports digital identity ecosystems is through identity federation. Identity federation allows users to authenticate once and gain access to multiple services without needing to manage multiple sets of credentials. This is particularly beneficial in environments where users interact with interconnected services, such as healthcare networks, financial institutions, and government agencies. Federation reduces friction in authentication processes while enhancing security by limiting the number of credentials a user needs to manage.

CIAM also plays a key role in decentralized identity models, where users control their identity data instead of relying on centralized databases. Decentralized identity, powered by blockchain technology and self-sovereign identity (SSI) principles, enables users to store and manage their credentials in digital wallets. CIAM solutions that support decentralized identity allow businesses to verify user credentials without storing sensitive data, reducing the risk of identity theft and data breaches. This approach aligns with emerging privacy regulations and enhances user trust by giving individuals greater control over their digital identities.

A well-implemented CIAM system ensures that digital identity ecosystems remain secure by incorporating adaptive authentication and risk-based access control. Instead of applying the same security policies to all users, CIAM evaluates contextual factors such as device reputation, geolocation, behavioral biometrics, and past login history to determine authentication requirements dynamically. If a login attempt appears suspicious, step-up authentication measures, such as requiring biometric verification or a one-time passcode (OTP), are triggered to prevent unauthorized access.

CIAM enhances trust within digital identity ecosystems by providing verifiable credentials that organizations can use to authenticate users across multiple platforms. Verifiable credentials, issued by trusted authorities such as government agencies or financial institutions, enable businesses to streamline identity verification while maintaining security and compliance. For example, a user who has already been verified by a financial institution can present a verifiable credential to another service provider, eliminating the need for repetitive identity verification processes.

Privacy and regulatory compliance are essential components of digital identity ecosystems, and CIAM ensures that businesses adhere to data protection laws such as the General Data Protection Regulation (GDPR), the California Consumer Privacy Act (CCPA), and industry-specific compliance requirements. CIAM solutions provide built-in consent management tools, allowing users to control how their personal data is collected, shared, and processed. By enabling transparent consent management, businesses build trust with users and demonstrate compliance with legal requirements.

Another way CIAM supports digital identity ecosystems is through secure API authentication and authorization. As businesses increasingly rely on API-driven architectures to connect services and share identity data, CIAM ensures that APIs are protected from unauthorized access and cyber threats. OAuth 2.0 and OIDC enable secure authentication for APIs, ensuring that only verified users and applications can access sensitive identity information. By implementing API security measures such as token-based authentication, rate limiting, and anomaly detection, CIAM helps prevent identity-related fraud and unauthorized data access.

CIAM solutions also improve user experience by enabling seamless identity synchronization across multiple digital platforms. A well-integrated CIAM system ensures that users can log in once and access all their services without encountering authentication barriers. This is particularly valuable in omnichannel environments where customers expect consistency between web applications, mobile apps, and IoT devices. Businesses that implement CIAM effectively provide a frictionless authentication experience, improving customer retention and engagement.

In the context of smart cities and digital government services, CIAM enables citizens to access public services securely while maintaining privacy. Governments implementing digital identity ecosystems rely on CIAM to authenticate users for online tax filing, healthcare services, and digital voting systems. By leveraging identity federation and verifiable credentials, public sector organizations provide citizens with seamless access to multiple government services without requiring them to manage multiple credentials.

Financial institutions also benefit from CIAM's role in digital identity ecosystems by enabling secure identity verification for online banking, digital payments, and financial transactions. Strong customer authentication (SCA) requirements under regulations such as the Revised Payment Services Directive (PSD2) mandate that financial institutions implement MFA and risk-based authentication. CIAM ensures that these security measures are in place while minimizing friction for legitimate users. Additionally, CIAM facilitates open banking initiatives by enabling secure API-based identity verification between banks and third-party financial service providers.

The healthcare industry relies on CIAM to support digital identity ecosystems that manage patient identities across multiple providers and platforms. CIAM ensures that patient records remain secure while allowing authorized healthcare professionals to access medical history, prescriptions, and treatment plans. Secure identity verification reduces the risk of medical identity fraud while enabling interoperability between electronic health record (EHR) systems.

As digital identity ecosystems continue to expand, businesses must adopt CIAM solutions that are flexible, scalable, and aligned with emerging security and privacy trends. CIAM not only protects digital identities but also facilitates seamless interactions between users, service providers, and regulatory authorities. Organizations that implement CIAM effectively strengthen digital trust, enhance security, and enable frictionless access across interconnected identity networks.

CIAM and Customer Trust: Building a Secure Relationship

Customer Identity and Access Management (CIAM) plays a crucial role in establishing and maintaining trust between businesses and their customers. In a digital landscape where personal information is constantly at risk, customers expect organizations to protect their data while ensuring a seamless and convenient experience. Trust is a key differentiator in today's competitive market, and businesses that fail to prioritize identity security risk losing customers to competitors that provide better protection and transparency.

One of the foundational elements of customer trust is secure authentication. Customers want to know that their accounts and personal data are safe from unauthorized access. Weak authentication mechanisms, such as reliance on passwords alone, create vulnerabilities that cybercriminals exploit through phishing, credential stuffing, and brute-force attacks. Implementing strong authentication measures, including multi-factor authentication (MFA), biometric authentication, and passwordless login, enhances security while reassuring customers that their identities are protected. Adaptive authentication, which adjusts security measures based on contextual risk factors, further strengthens trust by ensuring that authentication remains both secure and user-friendly.

Transparency is another essential factor in building customer trust. Users need to understand how their personal information is being collected, stored, and used. A well-implemented CIAM solution includes clear consent management, allowing customers to control their data-sharing preferences. Organizations must provide easy-to-understand privacy policies, explicit opt-in mechanisms, and the ability for users to modify or revoke consent at any time. When businesses are transparent about their data practices, customers feel more in control and are more likely to trust the organization with their personal information.

Protecting customer data from breaches is a critical aspect of maintaining trust. High-profile data breaches have eroded confidence in digital services, making users more cautious about sharing their information. A strong CIAM system enforces data encryption, secure storage practices, and strict access controls to minimize the risk of unauthorized data exposure. Organizations that proactively invest in cybersecurity measures, conduct regular security audits, and implement real-time threat detection demonstrate their commitment to safeguarding customer information.

Fraud prevention also plays a major role in fostering trust. Customers expect businesses to take proactive steps to prevent fraudulent activity, such as account takeovers, fake account creation, and payment fraud. AI-driven fraud detection, behavioral biometrics, and risk-based authentication help identify suspicious activities before they result in financial loss or identity theft. When customers see that fraud prevention measures are in place, they gain confidence in the security of the platform and are more likely to continue engaging with the business.

A seamless user experience is just as important as security when it comes to building trust. Customers want secure authentication but not at the cost of convenience. Lengthy registration processes, complex password policies, and frequent reauthentication requests can frustrate users and lead to abandonment. A well-designed CIAM system balances security with usability by offering progressive profiling, social login, and Single Sign-On (SSO). These features allow customers to authenticate easily while ensuring that security is not compromised.

Trust is also reinforced through effective account recovery mechanisms. Customers who lose access to their accounts due to forgotten passwords or expired authentication methods need a reliable way to regain control. CIAM solutions should provide secure and user-friendly recovery options, such as biometric verification, email-based recovery links, or customer support verification. If users struggle with account recovery or experience delays, their trust in the organization diminishes, and they may consider switching to a competitor with a more user-friendly system.

Regulatory compliance is another pillar of customer trust. With data protection laws such as the General Data Protection Regulation (GDPR), the California Consumer Privacy Act (CCPA), and the Payment Card Industry Data Security Standard (PCI DSS) in place, organizations are required to implement strict identity security measures. Customers are becoming increasingly aware of their data privacy rights and expect businesses to comply with legal frameworks. A CIAM solution that supports compliance ensures that businesses meet regulatory requirements while reassuring customers that their data is handled responsibly.

Personalization is another factor that can enhance customer trust when implemented correctly. Businesses that collect customer data for personalized experiences must do so ethically and transparently. Customers appreciate relevant recommendations, personalized marketing, and tailored content, but they also expect organizations to respect their privacy. A CIAM system that enables user-controlled personalization settings allows customers to decide how much data they want to share, fostering a sense of control and trust.

Cross-channel consistency is another trust-building factor in CIAM. Customers interact with businesses across multiple platforms, including websites, mobile apps, call centers, and in-store kiosks. A consistent identity experience across all channels reassures users that their information is secure and accessible regardless of how they engage with the brand. CIAM solutions that provide unified identity management ensure that users can authenticate seamlessly across different touchpoints without encountering inconsistencies or security gaps.

Communication is key in maintaining trust, especially when security incidents occur. Even the most secure systems can be targeted by cyberattacks, and how an organization responds to security threats significantly impacts customer confidence. Proactive security notifications, real-time alerts, and transparent breach disclosures help customers stay informed and take necessary precautions. A CIAM system that supports automated alerts for login attempts, suspicious activities, and policy updates ensures that customers remain aware of their account security status.

Trust is not a one-time achievement but an ongoing process. Businesses must continuously monitor, analyze, and improve their CIAM strategies to adapt to emerging security threats and evolving customer expectations. Regular security updates, continuous authentication improvements, and AI-driven identity protection help organizations stay ahead of cyber threats while ensuring that customers feel secure using their digital services.

By integrating CIAM with a trust-centric approach, businesses can foster long-term relationships with customers, reduce churn, and differentiate themselves in the marketplace. A secure, transparent, and user-friendly identity management system enhances customer confidence, making them more likely to engage with and remain loyal to a brand. Organizations that prioritize both security and usability in their CIAM strategy build not only a strong identity framework but also a lasting foundation of trust with their customers.

Automating CIAM Processes for Scalability

As businesses expand their digital presence and customer bases grow, Customer Identity and Access Management (CIAM) systems must be designed to handle increasing authentication requests, account creations, and access controls efficiently. Scalability is a critical factor in CIAM success, ensuring that authentication services remain responsive, secure, and reliable as demand fluctuates. Automation plays a key role in achieving scalability by reducing manual intervention, optimizing identity workflows, and improving security without compromising user experience.

One of the primary challenges organizations face in scaling CIAM is managing a growing number of authentication requests without introducing latency or downtime. Automated authentication workflows allow businesses to handle millions of login attempts seamlessly. By leveraging cloud-native CIAM solutions with auto-scaling capabilities, organizations can dynamically allocate resources based on traffic volume. This ensures that peak demand periods, such as holiday sales events or product launches, do not overwhelm authentication systems.

User registration and onboarding are key CIAM processes that benefit significantly from automation. A manual registration process requiring identity verification through human review can slow down onboarding and frustrate customers. Automated identity verification, including document scanning, biometric authentication, and AI-driven fraud detection, allows businesses to verify user identities in real time. Instead of requiring users to wait for manual approval, automated systems instantly validate government-issued IDs, compare biometric data, and cross-check third-party identity databases, reducing friction and improving conversion rates.

Adaptive authentication is another area where automation enhances scalability. Traditional static authentication methods apply uniform security measures to all users, regardless of risk level. Automated risk-based authentication dynamically adjusts security requirements based on factors such as device reputation, login history, geolocation, and behavioral patterns. If a login attempt is deemed low-risk, the system grants access with minimal friction. However, if the system detects anomalies—such as an unusual device or location—it automatically triggers step-up authentication, requiring additional verification. This automated approach ensures that security measures scale with user behavior while maintaining a seamless experience.

Password management is a common challenge in CIAM, with high volumes of password reset requests placing strain on IT and support teams. Automating passwordless authentication methods eliminates the need for users to remember complex passwords while reducing operational overhead. Magic links, biometric authentication, and passkeys provide secure, automated alternatives to traditional password-based authentication. Self-service password recovery mechanisms, including automated email and SMS-based account recovery, further reduce the need for human intervention, allowing users to regain account access quickly and securely.

Consent management is another critical CIAM function that benefits from automation. Regulatory requirements such as the General Data Protection Regulation (GDPR) and the California Consumer Privacy Act (CCPA) mandate that businesses obtain and manage user consent for data collection and processing. Manually tracking user consent across multiple platforms is inefficient and prone to errors. Automated consent management systems record user preferences in real time, updating databases and ensuring compliance across digital services. Customers can modify or revoke consent at any time, with changes instantly reflected across integrated platforms.

Fraud detection and identity threat prevention require automated monitoring and response mechanisms to scale effectively. AI-powered CIAM solutions analyze authentication patterns, detect anomalies, and identify suspicious activities without requiring manual review. Behavioral biometrics, such as keystroke dynamics and device fingerprinting, allow automated systems to recognize legitimate users based on unique interaction patterns. When potential fraud is detected, automated workflows trigger security measures such as temporary account locks, additional authentication steps, or fraud investigation alerts. This approach allows businesses to detect and mitigate threats in real time without overwhelming security teams.

Automating CIAM processes also improves customer support efficiency. Many authentication-related issues, such as account recovery, MFA setup, and session expirations, generate high volumes of support tickets. Automated chatbot assistants and self-service portals provide users with step-by-step guidance, reducing reliance on human agents. Automated identity verification during customer support interactions further enhances security by ensuring that only verified users can access account-related services.

Scalability also depends on secure API integration, as CIAM platforms interact with third-party applications, business partners, and cloud services. Automated API authentication and access controls ensure that only authorized applications can interact with CIAM systems. OAuth 2.0 and OpenID Connect (OIDC) provide standardized, automated token-based authentication for APIs, reducing the risk of credential exposure and unauthorized access. Automated monitoring tools track API authentication activity, detecting anomalies and enforcing security policies in real time.

Session management is another aspect of CIAM that benefits from automation. Automated session timeout policies ensure that inactive sessions are terminated securely, reducing the risk of unauthorized access. Continuous authentication mechanisms use AI-driven monitoring to detect anomalies during active sessions, triggering automatic reauthentication if suspicious behavior is detected. These automated security measures allow businesses to maintain session integrity at scale without requiring constant user intervention.

Businesses with multiple brands, franchises, or partner networks require federated identity management, which can be complex to manage manually. Automated identity federation streamlines authentication across different digital properties by allowing users to log in once and gain access to multiple services without reauthentication. Automating identity synchronization ensures that user attributes remain consistent across all connected platforms, reducing discrepancies and access errors.

Cloud-based CIAM solutions enhance automation by providing centralized identity management with global scalability. Automated provisioning and deprovisioning of user accounts ensure that employees, partners, and customers receive the appropriate access rights based on predefined policies. When users leave an organization or change roles, automated workflows revoke unnecessary access, reducing the risk of security vulnerabilities associated with inactive accounts.

Automated reporting and compliance tracking further enhance scalability by reducing the burden of manual audits. CIAM solutions generate real-time logs of authentication attempts, consent updates, and access control changes. These automated reports ensure regulatory compliance while providing security teams with visibility into identity-related activities. Businesses can configure automated alerts for unusual authentication patterns, policy violations, or potential security threats, enabling proactive risk mitigation.

As businesses continue to expand their digital presence, CIAM automation becomes a necessity for handling increasing authentication demands, improving security, and ensuring compliance. By leveraging AI-driven fraud detection, adaptive authentication, passwordless login, and automated identity verification, organizations can scale their CIAM systems without compromising user experience. Investing in automation ensures that businesses remain agile, secure, and prepared to meet the evolving challenges of digital identity management at scale.

Final Thoughts: The Road Ahead for CIAM

Customer Identity and Access Management (CIAM) has evolved into a cornerstone of digital security, user experience, and compliance in the modern business landscape. As organizations continue to embrace digital transformation, the role of CIAM will become even more integral in securing customer interactions while delivering seamless access to online services. The future of CIAM will be shaped by advancements in authentication technologies, regulatory changes, and the increasing need for frictionless digital experiences.

One of the primary drivers of CIAM's evolution is the growing adoption of passwordless authentication. Traditional passwords have long been a security liability, leading to widespread credential breaches and user frustration. Businesses are now shifting towards authentication mechanisms such as biometrics, magic links, and passkeys, which eliminate the need for users to remember and manage complex passwords. This transition enhances security while reducing friction in the authentication process, leading to higher user retention and satisfaction.

The rise of decentralized identity is another significant trend that will influence the future of CIAM. Traditional identity management models rely on centralized repositories, which are attractive targets for cybercriminals. Decentralized identity frameworks, built on blockchain technology and self-sovereign identity (SSI) principles, give users greater control over their personal information. Instead of storing credentials in a single database, users can manage their identity attributes in secure digital wallets, sharing only the necessary information with service providers. This model reduces the risk of data breaches while empowering individuals to take ownership of their digital identities.

Artificial intelligence (AI) and machine learning (ML) will continue to play a critical role in adaptive authentication and fraud prevention. AI-driven behavioral biometrics, which analyze how users interact with devices and applications, enable CIAM systems to detect anomalies and assess authentication risks in real time. By continuously learning from user behavior patterns, AI-powered CIAM solutions can distinguish between legitimate users and malicious actors, reducing false positives and improving security. AI also enhances fraud detection by identifying suspicious activities, such as credential stuffing, account takeovers, and synthetic identity fraud, before they cause damage.

The increasing complexity of regulatory requirements will shape how organizations implement CIAM. Privacy regulations such as GDPR, CCPA, and emerging global data protection laws are forcing businesses to rethink how they collect, store, and process customer identity data. CIAM platforms must include built-in compliance tools that facilitate consent management, data minimization, and transparent privacy policies. As regulations evolve, businesses will need to ensure that their identity management practices remain adaptable to new legal requirements while maintaining a high level of customer trust.

The need for seamless omnichannel experiences will push organizations to refine their CIAM strategies. Customers expect consistency across web applications, mobile apps, call centers, smart devices, and even in-person interactions. Businesses that implement federated identity management and Single Sign-On (SSO) will create a unified experience, allowing customers to authenticate once and access multiple services without repeated logins. The future of CIAM will focus on delivering cross-platform identity synchronization, ensuring that users can move between devices and applications effortlessly.

The integration of CIAM with the Internet of Things (IoT) will also become increasingly important. As IoT adoption grows, businesses must secure device identities just as they secure human identities. Connected devices, ranging from smart home assistants to industrial IoT sensors, require authentication mechanisms that prevent unauthorized access and data breaches. CIAM solutions must evolve to support device identity management, ensuring that only authorized devices can interact with sensitive systems and networks.

Cybersecurity threats will continue to evolve, making Zero Trust security principles a fundamental aspect of CIAM. The traditional perimeter-based security model is no longer sufficient in a world where users and devices connect from various locations. Zero Trust mandates continuous verification of identity, applying dynamic risk assessments to every access request. CIAM solutions will need to incorporate real-time security analytics, continuous authentication, and risk-based access controls to ensure that only trusted users and devices gain access to critical services.

The future of CIAM will also be shaped by advancements in user experience (UX) and personalization. Customers expect frictionless interactions with businesses, and identity management should not be a barrier to engagement. Organizations will focus on optimizing authentication flows by leveraging progressive profiling, which collects user information gradually rather than overwhelming them with lengthy registration forms. Personalization features, such as adaptive authentication based on user preferences and behavioral patterns, will create more intuitive identity experiences.

As businesses adopt cloud-native architectures, CIAM solutions must support scalable, distributed identity management. Cloud-based CIAM platforms provide the flexibility to handle fluctuating authentication demands while ensuring high availability and resilience. Organizations will continue migrating to cloud-based identity solutions, reducing dependency on on-premises infrastructure and enabling seamless integration with third-party services, APIs, and partner ecosystems.

The convergence of identity and cybersecurity will further drive the evolution of CIAM. Identity Threat Detection and Response (ITDR) will become a key focus, allowing organizations to detect and mitigate identity-based threats in real time. CIAM solutions will integrate with Security Information and Event Management (SIEM) and Extended Detection and Response (XDR) platforms, enhancing threat intelligence and automated incident response. As cybercriminals develop more sophisticated attack methods, businesses will need to leverage AI-driven identity analytics to detect compromised accounts, insider threats, and emerging security risks.

Looking ahead, organizations must adopt future-proof CIAM strategies that align with evolving technologies, regulatory changes, and customer expectations. Businesses that prioritize secure, seamless, and privacy-first identity management will gain a competitive advantage by fostering trust, enhancing security, and delivering superior user experiences. The next phase of CIAM will focus on balancing innovation with security, ensuring that digital identity ecosystems remain resilient in an increasingly complex digital world.